CHICKEN
AND POULTRY COOKBOOK

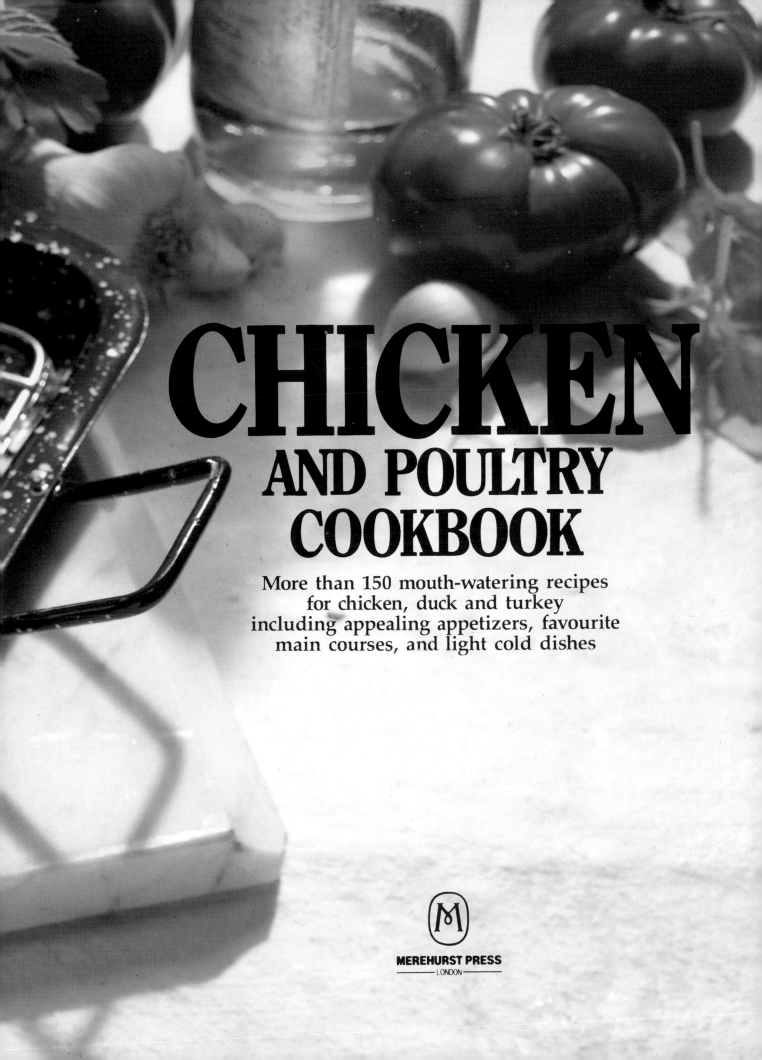

CHICKEN
AND POULTRY
COOKBOOK

More than 150 mouth-watering recipes
for chicken, duck and turkey
including appealing appetizers, favourite
main courses, and light cold dishes

MEREHURST PRESS
LONDON

Published 1990 Merehurst Limited
Ferry House
51/57 Lacy Road
Putney
London
SW15 1PR

Text by Marianne Kalenbach
Photographs by Fotostudio Teubner

Printed in Hong Kong

ISBN: 1-85391-121-6

Contents

Tips for Cooking Poultry

Drawing Poultry

A bird that is not oven-ready has to be drawn.

If there are any small feathers left after plucking, hold the bird over an open flame (of a gas burner or a lighted taper) turning it quickly. This will singe the feathers.

Chicken Portions

For many casseroles individual pieces are required. A small chicken cuts into 4 portions, a heavier bird into 6, and a duck, goose, or turkey into 8–12 portions.

Cut the thigh at the joint, where attached to the body. The leg and thigh may also be separated at the joint.

Boning a Chicken Breast

Start boning at the neck.

Cut the skin at the neck, peel it back.

Stuffing Poultry

Never overstuff the body cavity or the neck of a bird. Stuffing expands as it cooks.

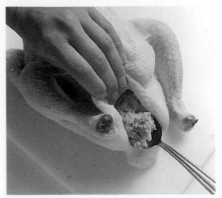

When filling the body cavity leave a space for closing the bird.

Cut head and neck off; pull out the gullet, windpipe, and gizzard. Cut off the feet at the first joint of the leg.

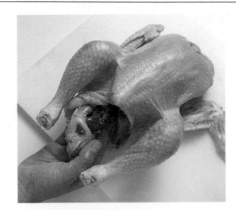

Cut across the rump, and remove the entrails. Rub one tablespoon salt into the inside of the carcass and wash out with water.

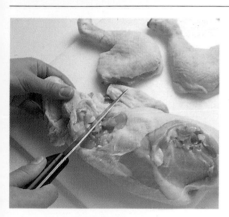

In a big bird the thigh is cut into two pieces.

Ease the breast in half, having cut through it lengthways with poultry scissors or a sharp knife. The back and small discarded pieces can be used for soup or sauce.

Cut through the breastbone lengthways.

Ease the flesh off the bone. Cut into fillets, and gently remove any skin by hand.

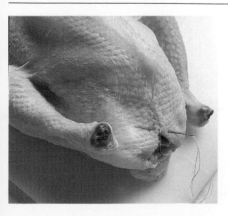

Both openings should be sewn together with a thick darning needle, and kitchen string. Close the opening from the back down, and sew across.

The opening can also be closed with wooden cocktail sticks.

Tips for Cooking Poultry

Trussing

The object of trussing is to keep the bird in good shape, thus making it easy to carve.

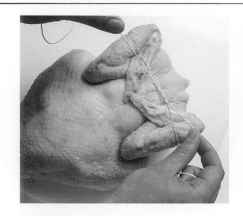

Fold the wings back neatly over the back of the carcass. Push a needle threaded with string through the carcass and tie back over the folded wings.

To Prevent Burning

Young poultry, without much fat, can easily burn during cooking.

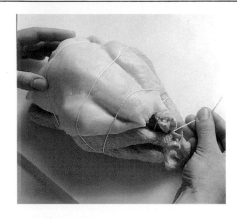

Before trussing place rashers of bacon over the breast, and tie in place securely.

Cooking on a Spit

Poultry cooked on a spit must be neatly trussed to turn easily.

A large chicken can hinder the rotation of the shaft on a rotisserie.

To Casserole Poultry

The bird should be covered in stock or water, on low heat. Add spices to the trussed bird, and leave it to simmer for 1½ hours.

Add vegetables, cloves, bay leaves, onion slices and parsley. Bring to the boil and skim off any froth that rises to the top.

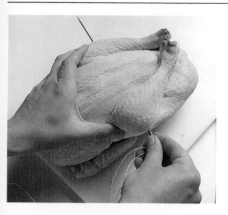

Likewise insert a large needle and string through the middle of the bird and tie at the top keeping the legs in place.

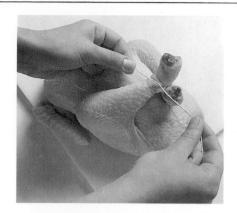

Or, tie the two legs together over the breast.

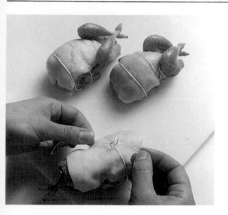

With very small birds, cover the entire breast with pieces of bacon fat. Secure with string.

For festive occasions weave 1 in/2 cm wide rashers of fat like a mat over the bird and fix securely in place.

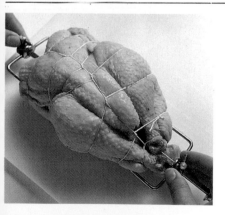

Securely fix the bird to the shaft or spit with holding forks to prevent it from roasting unevenly through not rotating properly.

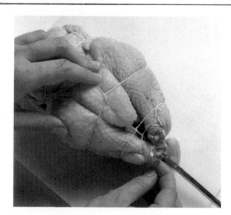

Size is not important when cooking over wood or coal.

Half-cover with lid and simmer gently. Never allow chicken to boil vigorously.

When adding vegetables, allow 2 medium sized carrots per person and 2 well-washed leeks tied up in a bundle per person.

Stuffings

Apple and Chestnut Stuffing

This stuffing is for many families the traditional Christmas stuffing for turkey and goose. It also goes very well with duck and wild duck. Chestnuts can be replaced with stoned prunes soaked in a little dry white wine. To stretch the filling for bigger birds use toasted white bread cubes and chopped almonds. For game birds the apples can be replaced by halved grapes without any pips. The following quantities are enough for a medium-sized bird:

Peel, core and cut 500 g/ 18 oz cooking apples into wedges and marinate in dry red wine until the apples look slightly pink. This takes approximately hours.

Minced Meat Stuffing

This stuffing goes well with most poultry. It is especially useful for increasing serving capacity. With fatty birds, use a veal, lamb or lean minced beef stuffing; whereas for lean birds, mixed minced meat or minced pork can be used. To make this stuffing lighter use soaked bread rolls or breadcrumbs and eggs, mixed with the chopped giblets and herbs. Our recipe:

Soak 1 or 2 stale bread rolls in cold water. Chop shallots and fry until golden brown. Squeeze the bread rolls dry and mix with 300–500 g/ 11–18 oz minced meat, eggs, the shallots, ½ tsp salt, pinch of dried mixe herbs, pinch of ground coriander. Mix to a mois but firm consistency.

Bread Stuffing

This stuffing is usually recommended when poultry is being eaten with only vegetables or a salad. While this stuffing might not be considered very interesting, it can be piquantly seasoned and combined with unusual ingredients. Suggestions for stuffing mixtures are: dried fruit soaked in wine, freshly chopped herbs, roasted and chopped almonds, sultanas, pickled root ginger, roasted sesame or sunflower seeds, chopped ham or chopped and lightly fried chicken liver. Our recipe:

Depending on the size o the bird, grate 3 or 4 sta bread rolls with a square grater. Alternatively, cut the bread rolls in half an soak in a light white win

Buckwheat Stuffing

This stuffing makes a very nutritious and substantial meal, with no need for rich accompaniments. Season the filling to taste and add ingredients with distinct flavours. Mushrooms, garlic, freshly chopped herbs, sweet–corn, spinach, celery, and onions are particularly good. You can also use rice (brown rice, wild rice), or par-boiled red lentils instead of the buckwheat for this stuffing. Our recipe:

Roast approximately 250 g/9 oz buckwheat in dry skillet until golden brown, stirring constantl Allow to cool.

Nick 500 g/18 oz chestnuts with a sharp knife and bake them in 250 ml/8 fl oz/1 cup water in oven at 220°C/425°F/Gas Mark 7 for 30 minutes until the skins crack. After 10 minutes pour 250 ml/8 fl oz/1 cup of cold water on the baking tray, to prevent the chestnuts from drying out. Peel the slightly cooled chestnuts and mix with the drained apples.

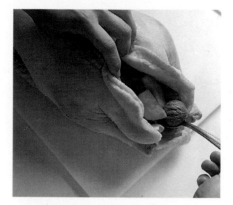

Mix 125 ml/4 fl oz/½ cup of oil with a pinch of white pepper and paprika and rub into the skin and inside of the bird. Rub the inside with ½ tsp salt. Stuff the bird with the apple and chestnut filling. Sew up the openings with thread and frequently baste the bird during cooking with the seasoned oil. Finally brush the bird with red wine.

Thinly slice the liver and heart, if desired. Fry in bubbling butter for 3 minutes, stirring constantly. Then mix with 2 tbsp of chopped chives and the minced meat mixture.

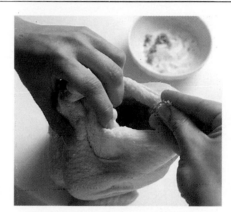

Rub the poultry with a mixture of a pinch of salt, dried herbs and ground coriander. Then stuff the bird with the minced meat stuffing. Sew up the openings, truss and roast the bird until crisp and golden brown.

Fry 100–150 g/4–5 oz chopped ham in bubbling butter for 3 minutes, stirring constantly, together with 50 g/2 oz each sliced mushrooms and chopped chicken livers.

Squeeze the bread rolls dry and mix with salt, pepper, 1 tsp chopped ginger, 2 tbsp soy sauce, 2 tbsp chopped and roasted almonds and 1–2 eggs. Combine with the mushroom mixture and stuff the bird. Before completion of cooking (about 15–30 minutes before), brush the bird with the white wine left from soaking the bread rolls.

Clean 2 celery sticks, several onions and 2 garlic cloves, chop and fry in butter until the onions are transparent. Add the buckwheat and 125–250 ml/4–8 fl oz/½–1 cup white wine, cover and lightly simmer for 5 minutes.

Mix the stuffing with 1 tsp freshly chopped thyme, 1 tbsp sesame oil and enough flour to bind the stuffing. Season the mixture with salt, add dried thyme and fold in 2 stiffly beaten egg whites.

Recommended Cooking Times

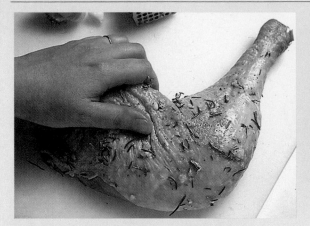

1) Before cooking, rub any spices into the washed and well-dried flesh, to penetrate the skin.

2) During roasting of large fatty birds, pierce the skin with a thin skewer to release the fat.

3) Small birds (or portions) cooked in a marinade need to be basted often during roasting to prevent them from drying out.

	Boil	Casseroling Whole Birds	Casseroling Portions	Roast
Poussins 300–500 g/ 11–18 oz (Aus 3–5)		50 minutes	30–50 minutes	180°C/350°F/Gas Mark 4 5 minutes then 160°C/325°F/Gas Mark 3 25 minutes (1 bird)
Spring Chicken 600–900 g/ 1¼–2 lbs (Aus 6–9)		1½ hours	40–50 minutes	180°C/350°F/Gas Mark 4 6 minutes then 160°C/325°F/Gas Mark 3 20 minutes per 450g/1 lb
Roasting Chicken 1–1.4 kg/ 2¼–3½ lbs (Aus 10–14)		1½ hours	45–60 minutes	180°C/350°F/Gas Mark 4 8 minutes then 160°C/325°F/Gas Mark 3 20 minutes per 450g/1 lb
Poulardes 1.3–1.6 kg/ 3–3¾ lbs (Aus 13–16)	1–1¾ hours	1½–2 hours	45–60 minutes	180°C/350°F/Gas Mark 4 25 minutes per 450 g/1 lb
Capon 1.5–2 kg/3½–4½ lbs (Aus 15–20)		2–3 hours	1 hour	(as for roasting chicken)
Boiling fowl for soup 1.7–2 kg/4–4½ lbs (Aus 17–20)	2 hours			
Guinea Fowl 800 g–1.25 kg/ 1¾–2½ lbs	1 hour	1½ hours	45–60 minutes	180°C/350°F/Gas Mark 4 20–25 minutes per 450 g/1 lb
Pigeon 300–400 g/ 11–14 oz	1 hour		30–50 minutes	
Young Duck 1.6–1.8 kg/ 3¾–4¼ lbs			50–70 minutes	180°C/350°F/Gas Mark 4 25–30 minutes per 450 g/1 lb
Duck 2–2.5 kg/4½–5½ lbs			1½–2 hours	(as above)
Goose 5–6 kg/11–13 lbs			2–3 hours	200°C/400°F/Gas Mark 6 15–17 minutes per 450 g/1 lb
Small Turkey 2–3 kg/4½–6½ lbs (Aus 20–30)		2½–3 hours	1½–2 hours	180°C/350°F/Gas Mark 4 20 minutes per 450 g/1 lb
Turkey 5 kg/11 lbs (Aus 50)			2½–3 hours	180°C/350°F/Gas Mark 4 15 minutes per 450 g/1 lb
Pheasant 1 kg/2¼ lbs	1 hour		45–60 minutes	
Partridge 100–400 g/4–14 oz			25–50 minutes	220°C/425°F/Gas Mark 7 20–25 minutes (1 bird)
Quail 100–200 g/4–7 oz		30–40 minutes	30–40 minutes	220°C/425°F/Gas Mark 7 15–20 minutes (1 bird)
Wild Duck 1–2 kg/2¼–4½ lbs	2 hours		1–1½ hours	(as for young duck)
Young Goose 4 kg/9 lbs			1¼–1½ hours	200°C/400°F/Gas Mark 6 17 minutes per 450 g/1 lb

A cooking chart is not foolproof. Cooking and roasting times are dependent on the age and quality of the bird and how long the oven will remain evenly heated. Therefore it is essential to check from time to time how the bird is cooking and to lower or raise the heat accordingly.

	Roast	Electric/Gas
Poussins 300–500 g/11–18 oz	Stuffed	220°C/425°F/Gas Mark 7 30 minutes
Spring Chicken 600–900 g/1 ¼–2 lbs (Aus 6–9)	Stuffed	220°C/425°F/Gas Mark 7 30–60 minutes
Roasting Chicken 1–1.4 kg/2¼–3½ lbs (Aus 10–14)	Stuffed	220°C/425°F/Gas Mark 7 1–1¾ hours
Poulardes 1.3–1.6 kg/3–3¾ lbs (Aus 13–16)	Stuffed	220°C/425°F/Gas Mark 7 1½–2 hours
Capon 1.5–2 kg/3½–4½ lbs (Aus 15–20)	Stuffed	220°C/425°F/Gas Mark 7 1¾–2¼ hours
Guinea Fowl 800–1.2 kg/1¾– 2½ lbs	Stuffed	200°C/425°F/Gas Mark 7 45 minutes–1¼ hours
Pigeon 300–400 g/11–14 oz	Stuffed	200°C/425°F/Gas Mark 7 30 minutes
Young Duck 1.6–1.8 kg/3¾–4¼ lbs	Stuffed	200°C/425°F/Gas Mark 7 2–2½ hours
Duck 2–2.5 kg/4½–5½ lbs	Stuffed	180°C/350°F/Gas Mark 4 2½–3¼ hours
Small Goose 4 kg/9 lbs	Stuffed	180°C/350°F/Gas Mark 4 3¾ hours
Goose 5–6 kg/ 11–13 lbs	Stuffed	180°C/350°F/Gas Mark 4 4½–5½ hours
Small Turkey 2–3 kg/ 4½–6½ lbs (Aus 20–30)	Stuffed	180°C/350°F/Gas Mark 4 1¾–2¾ hours
Turkey Hen 5 kg/ 11 lbs (Aus 50)	Stuffed	180°C/350°F/Gas Mark 4 3¾ hours
Pheasant 1 kg/2¼ lbs	Stuffed	220°C/425°F/Gas Mark 7 45–60 minutes
Partridge 100–400 g/4–14 oz	Stuffed	220°C/425°F/Gas Mark 7 15–20 minutes
Quail 100–200 g/4–7 oz	Stuffed	220°C/425°F/Gas Mark 7 10–15 minutes
Wild Duck 4 kg/9 lbs	Stuffed	180°C/350°F/Gas Mark 4 5¼ hours

4) To make a crispy finish, brush the skin with a marinade of salt, honey and water, beer or wine about 15–30 minutes before a large bird has finished roasting.

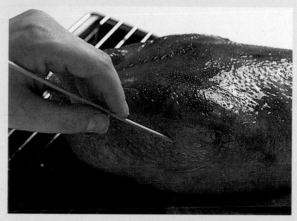

5) To prevent overcooking, pierce the skin from time to time until the juices are no longer a red or rosy colour, beginning about two-thirds of the way through cooking.

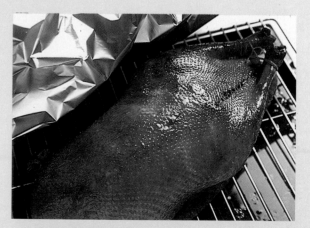

6) About 10 minutes before carving, cover the bird loosely with foil and keep warm.

Soups and Stews

Chicken Consommé with Tiny Dumplings

Quick and simple to make

Preparation and cooking time: 30 minutes
Serves 4

500 g/18 oz chicken breast
2 shallots
1 tsp salt
Pinch white pepper
Pinch dried thyme
10 tbsp fine breadcrumbs
1 tbsp chopped parsley
1 egg
4 tbsp single (light) cream
1 litre/2 pt/5 cups chicken stock
300 g/11 oz frozen peas

Mince the meat finely, either in a mincer or a food-processor. • Peel shallots and chop very finely before mixing them with the chicken, salt, pepper, thyme, breadcrumbs, parsley and egg, with sufficient cream to form a soft pliable dough. • Bring the stock to the boil with the peas, reduce heat to simmer gently. • Shape the chicken mixture into little dumplings, using 2 teaspoons dipped in cold water. Put dumplings into simmering stock and cook gently for 10 minutes. • Serve soup immediately.

Chicken Consommé

Economical but impressive

Thawing time: 4 hours
Preparation time: 10 minutes
Cooking time: 2 hours
Serves 4

1 kg/2¼ lbs frozen chicken giblets
2 litres/4 pt/10 cups water
2 tsp salt
1 leek
2 carrots
2 sprigs celery tops
2 sprigs parsley
2 small onions
1 bay leaf
1 clove
4 white peppercorns
4 egg yolks
2 tbsp chopped chives

Remove giblets from wrapping and allow to thaw in a sieve placed over a bowl. Pour away any water that collects during the process. • Wash the giblets, put into a large saucepan with the water and salt. Bring to the boil. Turn down the heat so that the stock barely simmers. Skim off any scum that forms during the first 30 minutes. Simmer gently for another hour, until the stock is reduced by half. • Meanwhile, wash the leek, removing the green part, and cut lengthwise into strips. Scrape and wash the carrots and cut into rounds. Wash the celery tops and herbs, peel the onions and spike the bay leaf into it with the clove. • Add prepared vegetables and peppercorns to stock after it has simmered for the first hour and a half, cover the pan and simmer 30 minutes longer. • Put one egg yolk into each of 4 soup bowls. Pour the stock through a fine sieve or a piece of muslin. If you wish to remove all fat from the stock it must be left to cool; then the solidified fat can be removed and the consommé reheated. Pour the consommé over the egg yolk in each soup bowl and serve sprinkled with chives.

Tip: The leek and carrot may be finely chopped and served in the consommé.

Cream of Chicken Soup

A family favourite

Preparation time: 40 minutes
Cooking time: 2 hours
Serves 4

1 boiling chicken weighing 1 kg/ 2¼ lbs
2 litres/4 pt/10 cups water
2 tsp salt
3 leeks
1 large carrot
1 stick celery
2 small onions
1 bay leaf
2 cloves
4 white peppercorns
40 g/2 oz butter
3 tbsp plain flour
2 egg yolks
125 ml/4 fl oz/½ cup double (thick) cream

Wash chicken thoroughly inside and out, bring to the boil with water and salt, and reduce heat until water simmers very gently. Skim off any scum that forms during the first 30 minutes. • Simmer for 2 hours altogether, until stock is reduced by a good half. • Remove green leaves from leeks, wash white part thoroughly. Peel, wash and slice carrot. Rinse celery and slice. Peel onions and spike bay leaf onto it with cloves. • After stock has simmered for 1½ hours, add prepared vegetables and peppercorns and simmer, covered, for remaining 30 minutes. • Lift chicken out of stock, slice breast meat and set aside. • Strain stock, allow to cool and remove fat. • Slice leeks. • Melt butter, add flour and gradually add 1 litre/2 pt stock and simmer gently for 10 minutes. • Add sliced chicken breast and leek to soup. • Beat egg yolks and cream together and use to thicken soup.

Delicate Chicken Soup

An Hungarian speciality

Preparation time: 30 minutes
Cooking time: 1½ hours
Serves 4

| 1 chicken weighing 1 kg/2¼ lbs |
| 1.5 litres/3 pt/6 cups water |
| Bunch flat-leaved parsley |
| 1 tsp salt |
| 2 cooking apples |
| 1 tsp honey |
| 1 tbsp oatmeal |
| 125 ml/4 fl oz/½ cup soured cream |
| 1 egg yolk |

Wash the chicken, cut into 8 pieces and bring to the boil in the water. Reduce heat so that stock barely simmers, continually skimming off any scum that forms during the first 30 minutes. • Rinse and dry the parsley, then chop the leaves and put to one side, covered. • Add the parsley stalks with the salt to the stock and simmer for 50 minutes longer. • Peel and quarter the apples, remove core and cut into thin slices before cooking gently in a covered saucepan with 4 tbsp water and the honey until they are just soft. • Remove parsley stalks and chicken pieces from stock, separate the meat from the skin and bones and chop it. • Toast the oatmeal to a light brown, stir into the soured cream and add to the stock. Simmer for 5 minutes more. • Add the cubed chicken and apple slices to the soup and reheat, then remove from the heat. • Whisk the egg yolk with 2 tbsp of the hot soup and use this to thicken the soup, before sprinkling with the chopped parsley.

Spicy Chicken Soup

Simple but delicious

Thawing time: 4 hours
Preparation time: 20 minutes
Cooking time: 1 hour
Serves 4

| 500 g/18 oz frozen chicken giblets |
| 1.5 litres/3 pt/6 cups water |
| 1 tsp salt |
| Mixed root vegetables |
| 2 small onions |
| 200 g/7 oz chicken breast, boned |
| 100 g/4 oz button mushrooms |
| 25g/1 oz butter |
| 1 tbsp curry powder |
| Pinch cayenne pepper |
| Chives |

Place the unwrapped chicken giblets in a sieve over a bowl to thaw, throwing away any water that collects in the process. • Wash the giblets thoroughly, place in a saucepan, cover with the water and bring to the boil. Remove any scum as it forms. • Add salt and vegetables and simmer gently for 1 hour. • Meanwhile, peel and finely chop onions, cut chicken breasts into thin strips, clean and slice mushrooms. • Heat butter in heavy skillet and fry chopped onion gently with chicken strips, turning frequently, until both are done. Add sliced mushrooms and fry 1 minute longer, then stir in curry powder and cayenne pepper. • Strain chicken stock over chicken strips and vegetables and keep hot. • Rinse chives before chopping finely and sprinkling over soup.

Cream of Chicken Soup with Banana

Economical and easy

Thawing time: 4 hours
Preparation time: 40 minutes
Cooking time: 1 hour, 10 minutes
Serves 4

---

500 g/18 oz frozen chicken giblets

1.5 litres/3 pt/6 cups water

1 tsp salt

Mixed root vegetables

2 small onions

50 g/2 oz butter

2 tbsp plain flour

1 cooking apple

2 bananas

4 tbsp double (thick) cream

2 tsp lemon juice

Pinch white pepper

1 tbsp flaked almonds

Unwrap giblets and allow to thaw, then wash them and bring to the boil in the water. Skim off scum as it forms. Add the salt and vegetables and simmer for 1 hour. • Strain the stock and take any meat off the bone. • Peel and chop onions, then fry in butter until transparent. Sprinkle with flour, continue to fry a little longer, then stir in stock gradually. Add meat. Simmer gently for 10 minutes longer. • Peel and finely grate the apple. Peel the bananas, mash one of them and mix into the soup together with the cream and grated apple. • Season to taste with lemon juice and pepper, serve garnished with sliced banana and toasted almond flakes.

Tip: Use 2 sliced carrots, 1 chopped turnip and a small cubed piece of swede for the root vegetables.

Cream of Chicken Soup with Asparagus

Wholefood recipe

Preparation time: 30 minutes
Cooking time: 1¾ hours
Serves 4

Soup vegetables (e.g. onion, leek, carrot, small piece of celery or celeriac, turnip)

½ small boiling chicken weighing 800 g/1¾ lbs

1.75 litres/3½ pt/7 cups water

1 bay leaf

5 white peppercorns

1 tsp sea salt

400 g/14 oz fresh asparagus

150 g/5 oz green peas, shelled

50 g/2 oz/½ cup wholewheat flour

250 ml/8 fl oz/1 cup single (light) cream

2 egg yolks

Pinch seasoning salt

Juice of ½ lemon

2 tbsp freshly chopped chervil

Prepare, wash and chop the soup vegetables in small pieces. • Wash the chicken, cover with the water and bring to the boil together with the soup vegetables, bay leaf and peppercorns. Add the salt. Simmer 1½ hours. • Wash the asparagus and peel the woody end thinly. Cut off the tips about 5 cm/2 in down and put aside. • Cut the remaining asparagus stalks into small pieces and add to the stock for the final 10 minutes of the cooking time. Strain the stock and measure out 1 litre/2 pt of it. Bring this to the boil again before adding the cooked asparagus pieces, asparagus tips and peas. Simmer 5 minutes more. • Take chicken meat off the bone, chop into pieces and add to the soup. • Mix the flour to a paste with 250 ml/8 fl oz/1 cup

cold stock, pour into soup, simmer gently for 5 minutes, stirring constantly, then remove from heat. • Beat the cream with egg yolks and use to thicken the soup. Season to taste with seasoning salt and lemon juice, sprinkle with chopped chervil.

Turkey and Vegetable Soup

Worth the time

Preparation time: 30 minutes
Cooking time: 1¼ hours
Serves 4

800 g/1¾ lbs turkey meat	
2 tbsp oil	
2 litres/4 pt/8 cups hot water	
1 tsp salt	
2 small onions	
1 celery stick	
2 carrots	
1 turnip	

150 g/5 oz each green beans, shelled peas and cauliflower florets	
Pinch white pepper	
1 tsp soy sauce	
Handful chervil	

Rinse and dry meat. Heat oil in a saucepan, add meat and brown evenly, add the water and salt and bring to the boil. • Peel onions, trim and slice celery, add to soup. Simmer for 1 hour. During first 30 minutes, remove any scum that forms, then almost cover pot with lid, allowing some steam to escape. • Peel and wash carrots; slice into thin rounds. Peel and chop turnip, wash beans and cut into pieces. • Take meat, onions and soup vegetables out of stock by pouring stock through a sieve. Return stock to pan, add carrots, turnip, beans, peas and cauliflower, and simmer for 15

minutes. • Chop meat. Wash and chop chervil. • Return meat to soup, heat through, season with salt, pepper and soy sauce and sprinkle with chopped chervil.

Pigeon Cream Soup

Delicate and unusual

Preparation time: 40 minutes
Cooking time: 1 hour
Serves 4

2 prepared pigeons weighing 400 g/14 oz each	
1.5 litres/2½ pt/6 cups water	
1 tsp salt	
Strip lemon peel	
2 small onions	
2 leeks	
Small piece celeriac	
Sprig each parsley, thyme and dill	
2 egg yolks	
5 tbsp double (thick) cream	

1 tbsp fresh dill	

Wash birds well inside and out, put into a large pot with the water, salt and lemon peel and simmer gently for 30 minutes. Skim off scum continuously as it forms. • Peel onions, cut in half, and place cut sides down in a dry frying pan to brown. • Take the white part of leeks only, wash and cut into fine strips. Peel, rinse and dice celeriac. Rinse herbs and tie together. • Add prepared vegetables and herbs to stock and continue to simmer, half-covered, for 30 minutes. By the end of this time the liquid should be reduced by half. • Strain the soup. Remove the skin and bones from the pigeons and chop the meat before returning it to the soup. Beat egg yolks with cream, combine with 3 tbsp hot stock and stir into soup. • Serve the soup sprinkled with dill.

Duck Soup in a Pastry Bonnet

Complicated, but wins compliments

Preparation time: 40 minutes
Baking time: 10 minutes
Serves 4

4 sheets frozen puff pastry, about 65 g/1½ oz each

250 g/9 oz duck breast

1 tsp oil

Pinch each salt and freshly ground black pepper

2 spring onions

250 g/9 oz courgettes (zucchini)

100 g/4 oz button mushrooms

250 ml/8 fl oz/1 cup strong chicken stock

150 g/5 oz mildly flavoured sausagemeat

Bunch chervil

4 tbsp single (light) cream

1 egg yolk

Thoroughly thaw puff pastry and set aside. • Wash and dry duck breast before browning the skin side in oil, then turning and completing the process in 3 minutes. Season with salt and pepper. • Trim and wash spring onions, then chop in rings. Wash, dry and dice courgettes (zucchini) finely. Clean and rinse mushrooms, then slice them. • Heat the chicken stock. • Put sausagemeat into a bowl, add the washed and finely chopped chervil, 2 tbsp cream and some pepper. Mix well and then shape with teaspoons into little dumplings and simmer gently in the stock for 10 minutes. • Cut the duck into fine strips and divide it together with the finely chopped vegetables among four soup bowls. • Preheat oven to 220°C/425°F/Gas Mark 7. • Roll pastry out to form circles 2 cm /¾ in bigger than the diameter of the bowls. Whisk egg yolk with remaining cream. • Fill bowls with hot soup and dumplings. Cover with a pastry lid and glaze with egg yolk. • Bake in centre of oven for about 10 minutes until pastry is well browned.

Ujhazy Chicken Soup

An Hungarian speciality

Preparation time: 30 minutes
Cooking time: 1¼ hours
Serves 4

| ½ boiling chicken weighing 800 g/1¾ lbs |
| 100 g/4 oz celeriac |
| 100 g/4 oz carrot |
| 100 g/4 oz cauliflower |
| 2 small onions |
| 1 garlic clove |
| 1½ tsp salt |
| 6 black peppercorns |
| 1 large tomato |
| 100 g/4 oz frozen peas |
| 50 g/2 oz vermicelli |

Wash chicken thoroughly. Scrape or peel celeriac and cut carrots into julienne strips. • Rinse cauliflower and break into florets. • Peel onions and garlic. • Cover fowl with cold water and bring to the boil, skimming off scum as it forms. • Add salt, peppercorns, and any whole pieces of celeriac and carrot, onions, garlic and quartered tomato to fowl and simmer for 1 hour. • Cook peas, cauliflower florets and julienne strips, covered, in small amount of water for 10 minutes, then strain. • Cook vermicelli for 3 minutes in 500 ml/16 fl oz/2 cups boiling water and drain. • Remove chicken from stock, separate meat from skin and bones, cut into small cubes and place with vermicelli and vegetables in a tureen. • Strain the soup over this mixture and serve.

Squire's Pheasant Soup

A Polish speciality

Preparation time: 45 minutes
Cooking time: 1½ hours
Serves 4

| 1 pheasant weighing 1 kg/2¼ lbs |
| 1½ tsp salt |
| 6 black peppercorns |
| 1 bay leaf |
| 1.5 litres/2½ pt/6 cups water |
| 1 celeriac |
| 2 carrots |
| 1 small leek |
| 3 tbsp sunflower oil |
| 1 tbsp plain flour |
| 125 ml/4 fl oz/½ cup soured cream |
| Bunch parsley |

Rinse pheasant, place in pan with salt, peppercorns, bay leaf and water and bring to the boil, repeatedly skimming off scum as it forms. • Continue to cook, uncovered, over gentle heat for 1 hour. • Remove cooked pheasant from stock. Strain stock. • Peel celeriac, scrape carrots, and slice thinly. Clean and rinse leek and cut into thin rounds. • Heat oil and brown prepared vegetables in it. • Sprinkle with flour, fry a little longer, then gradually stir in stock. Simmer soup for 10 minutes. • Discard skin and bones of pheasant and chop the meat. • Return meat to stock and reheat, then stir in soured cream. • Rinse and dry parsley thoroughly, then chop finely. • Serve soup sprinkled with chopped parsley.

Sapporo Chicken Soup

A luxurious Japanese soup

Preparation time: 45 minutes
Cooking time: 15 minutes
Serves 4

500 g/18 oz chicken breast fillets	
1 white radish (50 g/2 oz)	
1 small carrot (50 g/2 oz)	
200 g/7 oz potatoes	
1 leek, white part only (50 g/2 oz)	
200 g/7 oz green beans	
2 tbsp peanut oil	
1 litre/1¾ pt/4 cups rich chicken stock	
5 tbsp soy sauce	
2 tsp honey	
1–2 pinches salt	
1 tsp green peppercorns	
100 g/4 oz peeled prawns	

Rinse, pat dry and cube chicken fillets. • Scrape and rinse radish, then cut into strips the size of matchsticks. Scrape carrot and potatoes, rinse and dry, cut into similar strips. Repeat process with leek and green beans. • Heat peanut oil. Fry cubes of chicken in it, add vegetables and continue to fry for a few minutes, turning all the time. • Heat chicken stock and pour onto vegetables. Cover pot and simmer for 15 minutes, then season with soy sauce, honey, salt and green peppercorns. Finally add prawns and reheat gently.

Tip: If you can't get peanut oil, use sunflower oil instead.

Guinea Fowl Soup with Vegetables

A quick and easy classic

Preparation time: 30 minutes
Cooking time: 1 hour
Serves 4

1 guinea fowl weighing 800 g/1¾ lbs	
1 tsp salt	
1.5 litres/3 pt/6 cups water	
1 onion	
1 bay leaf	
1 clove	
500 g/18 oz courgettes (zucchini)	
1 bunch watercress	

Wash guinea fowl thoroughly, inside and out, put in pot with salt and water and bring to the boil. • In the meantime, peel onion and use the clove to spike the bay leaf into it. • During the first 30 minutes of cooking time, skim off any scum that forms. At the end of this time, add onion and simmer for 20 minutes until reduced by half. • Rinse, dry and cube courgettes (zucchini). Rinse and dry watercress thoroughly and remove any thick stalks. • Add chopped courgettes (zucchini) to the stock and cook for 10 minutes. • Lift guinea fowl and onions from stock. Allow liquid to simmer, covered, while preparing meat. • Take meat from bones, cut into pieces and return to soup. • Serve sprinkled with watercress.

Mulligatawny

An Anglo-Indian favourite

Preparation time: 35 minutes
Cooking time: about 45 minutes
Serves 4

100 g/4 oz/¾ cup long-grain rice
1.25 litres/2½ pt/5 cups chicken stock
500 g/18 oz skinned chicken breast fillets
1 carrot (100 g/4 oz)
1 leek, white part only (100 g/4 oz)
2 tbsp peanut oil
4 tbsp sultanas
1 cooking apple
1 tbsp curry powder
Good pinch cayenne pepper
2 tbsp desiccated coconut

Rinse rice in colander under running water until water runs clear. • Bring chicken stock to the boil, add rice and boil moderately fast, uncovered, for 20 minutes. • Cut chicken into small cubes. Scrape carrot and slice thinly. Wash leek thoroughly in warm water and slice into rounds. • Heat peanut oil in a large skillet. First fry chicken cubes until nicely browned, then remove from skillet and fry prepared vegetables in remaining oil. Add the chicken and vegetables, with as little oil as possible, to rice and stock. • Cover sultanas with hot water, changing water as necessary, until nice and plump. • Strain. Rinse, dry, peel and grate apple, then add to soup with sultanas. • Season soup to taste with curry powder and cayenne pepper and sprinkle with coconut before serving.

Chicken and Rice Stew

Economical and simple to prepare

Preparation time: 30 minutes
Cooking time: 1 hour and 20 minutes
Serves 4

1.5 litres/2½ pt/5 cups water
1 chicken weighing 1 kg/2¼ lbs
Sprig each tarragon, parsley, celery leaves and thyme
1 leek, white part only (100 g/4 oz)
2 shallots
1 tsp salt
500 g/18 oz fresh peas
200 g/7 oz carrots
200 g/7 oz/1⅓ cups long-grain rice
Pinch cayenne pepper
2 tbsp chopped parsley

Bring water to the boil and cook cleaned chicken in it for 30 minutes, skimming off scum as it forms. • Rinse herbs and tie together; wash leek and slice into rounds. Peel and quarter shallots. • When chicken has simmered for 30 minutes, add herbs, leek, shallots and salt to pan, cover and cook for another 30 minutes. • Shell peas. Scrape, rinse and chop carrots. Put rice in a sieve and wash under cold running water until water runs clear. Drain. • Take chicken and herbs out of stock. Add vegetables and rice to stock, cover and simmer on low heat for 20 minutes. • Remove chicken meat from carcass and cut into small pieces, then return to pot. Season to taste with cayenne pepper and serve sprinkled with chopped parsley.

Chicken and Vegetable Stew

Simple to prepare and economical

Preparation and cooking time: 1¼ hours
Serves 4

1 chicken weighing 1 kg/2¼ lbs
Several small onions
1 carrot (100 g/4 oz)
2 leeks (200 g/7 oz)
75 g/3 oz butter
1 tsp salt
2 tsp paprika
2 pinches white pepper
250 ml/8 fl oz/1 cup pure, unsweetened apple juice
400 g/14 oz tomatoes
100 g/4 oz button mushrooms
2 tbsp chopped chives

Rinse chicken and cut into 8 pieces. • Peel onion, scrape carrot and chop both. Wash white part of leeks and slice. • Heat 50 g/2 oz of the butter in a large, heavy-bottomed pan. Fry chicken pieces, turning as necessary to brown well on all sides, then remove from skillet. • Brown chopped onions and carrot in the butter. Add remaining butter and leeks; fry briefly, then lay chicken pieces on bed of vegetables. Sprinkle the mixture with salt, paprika and pepper before pouring on apple juice. Cover and cook over low heat for 35 minutes. • Skin tomatoes and chop, removing core. • Clean and rinse mushrooms, cut into fine slices and add with tomatoes to the stew for the final 10 minutes of cooking time. • Serve stew sprinkled with chopped chives.

Chicken and Turnip Stew

Healthy and tasty

Preparation time: 45 minutes
Cooking time: 1 hour, 25 minutes
Serves 4

Assorted soup vegetables (including carrot, celeriac, leek, onion)

1 chicken weighing 1.2 kg/ 2½ lbs

1.5 litres/3 pt/6 cups water

2 tsp sea salt

5 white peppercorns

1 kg/2¼ lbs turnips, preferably young white ones

250 g/9 oz shallots

Bunch parsley

2 pinches each freshly ground black pepper and sea salt

Rinse, clean and finely chop soup vegetables. • Wash chicken thoroughly both inside and out. Put in pan with half the prepared soup vegetables, water, salt and peppercorns, and cook gently for 1 hour until tender. Remove any scum that forms during the first 30 minutes. • Peel and rinse turnips and cut into quarters lengthwise, then slice thinly. Peel and halve shallots. • Remove chicken from stock and discard vegetables. Cook turnips plus remaining soup vegetables and onions for 25 minutes in stock until done. • Take meat off bones and cut into good sized pieces. • Rinse parsley in lukewarm water, dry well, remove thick stalks and chop leaves finely. • Remove pan from heat. Stir chicken meat and parsley into soup and season to taste with pepper and salt. • Serve with slices of hearty rye bread.

Chicken Stew with Leeks and Carrots

Well worth the effort

Preparation time: 40 minutes
Cooking time: 2 hours, 10 minutes
Serves 4

500 g/18 oz carrots

3 celery stalks

400 g/14 oz leeks

2 small onions

2 garlic cloves

1.5 litres/2½ pt/6 cups water

Sprig fresh thyme

1 bay leaf

1 clove

2 tsp sea salt

1 tsp white peppercorns

1 boiling chicken weighing 1.8kg/ 4 lbs

2 young turnips

400 g/14 oz courgettes (zucchini)

Pinch white pepper

Scrape carrots and celery, wash together with leeks. Roughly chop 2 carrots, celery and 1 leek. • Peel and chop onions and garlic. Bring prepared vegetables to the boil in the water together with thyme, bay leaf, clove, salt and peppercorns. • Rinse fowl and add to water, skimming off any scum that forms during the first 30 minutes. • Cook chicken gently for an additional 1½ hours until tender. • Remove green leaves from remaining leeks and slice. Cut peeled turnips, rinsed courgettes (zucchini) and remaining carrots in julienne strips. Slice remaining leeks. • Remove chicken from stock. Strain stock, bring to the boil again and simmer vegetables in it for 10 minutes. • Separate meat from bones, cut in small cubes, return to pan and season to taste with salt and pepper.

Sweet and Sour Goose Stew

Unusual

Soaking time: 12 hours
Preparation time: 25 minutes
Cooking time: 1 hour, 10 minutes
Serves 4

200 g/7 oz/1⅓ cups mixed dried fruit

1 kg/2¼ lbs goose giblets (wings, neck, gizzard and heart)

250 ml/8 fl oz/1 cup water

1 onion

1 bay leaf

2 cloves

Soup vegetables, carrots, leeks, celeriac etc.

Salt

75g/3 oz butter

5 tbsp plain flour

2 tbsp cider vinegar

1 tbsp sugar

2 pinches black pepper

Cover dried fruit with water and soak for 12 hours. • Rinse goose giblets, bring to the boil in the water and skim off scum as it forms. • Peel the onion and spike the bay leaf into it with the cloves. Clean and rinse soup vegetables, add to pan with onion and a little salt. Cover and cook for 1 hour over gentle heat until reduced by one-third. • After 30 minutes of the cooking time, add dried fruit, along with the water it was soaked in. • Strain stock and measure out 500 ml/16 fl oz/2 cups. • Melt butter, brown flour in it, then gradually stir in stock and simmer for 10 minutes. • Season with vinegar, sugar, salt and pepper. • Add dried fruit and meaty pieces of goose to sauce and warm through. • Serve with bread dumplings.

Hungarian Chicken

A speciality from Eastern Europe

Preparation time: 1 hour
Cooking time: 2 hours
Serves 4

1 boiling chicken weighing 1.5 kg/3½ lbs

1½ tsp salt

2 litres/4 pt/8 cups water

Soup vegetables, carrots, leek, celery, etc.

100 g/4 oz streaky bacon

4 small onions

2 large tomatoes

2 green peppers

1 tbsp oil

2 tbsp paprika

Pinch each salt and freshly ground black pepper

Wash chicken and giblets, putting liver to one side. Bring to the boil with salt and water, removing scum as it forms. • Rinse and clean soup vegetables, add to chicken and cook for 1½ hours. • Finely chop bacon and onions. Skin and chop tomatoes. Halve peppers, removing seeds and white ribs, before drying and cutting into strips. • Strain chicken stock and measure off 500 ml/16 fl oz/2 cups. Divide chicken into 12 portions and discard giblets. • Heat oil and fry bacon, then brown chicken portions in bacon fat. Add onions and pepper and fry briefly. Stir in paprika and then chicken stock. Cook for 10 minutes. • Chop liver and add to pan with tomatoes, simmer gently for 10 minutes longer. Season to taste with salt and pepper.

Savoy Cabbage with Goose

An Italian speciality

Preparation time: 1 hour
Cooking time: 1½ hours
Serves 8

25 g/1 oz bacon	
3 medium carrots	
2 small onions	
1 kg/2¼ lbs Savoy cabbage	
1 young fat goose weighing 3 kg/6½ lbs	
25g/1 oz butter	
125 ml/4 fl oz/½ cup red Burgundy	
1 tsp salt	
2 pinches black pepper	
1 tbsp tomato purée (paste)	
125 ml/4 fl oz/½ cup chicken stock	

Chop bacon. Scrape and rinse carrots before slicing thinly. Peel onions, quarter them and cut in fine slices. • Cut cabbage into quarters, removing hard central core and any tough outer leaves. Rinse quarters and cut into thick slices. • Cut goose into 16 portions, wash and dry them. • Preheat oven to 180°C/350°F/Gas Mark 4. • Heat butter and bacon in a heavy-bottomed casserole. Brown goose portions thoroughly. Add onions and carrots and continue to fry for 10 more minutes. Remove breast portions and put to one side. • Add red wine, sliced cabbage, salt and pepper, mix well and fry a few minutes longer. • Combine tomato purée (paste) and chicken stock, pour over vegetables and cover casserole before placing in middle of oven. • Cook for 1½ hours, returning breast portions to the dish for the last 30 minutes.

Goose and Turnip Stew

A warming winter dish

Preparation and cooking time: 1½ hours
Serves 4

1 goose carcass	
600 g/1¼ lb roast goose	
Meat juices from roast	
500 ml/16 fl oz/2 cups water	
2 medium onions	
500 g/18 oz small white turnips	
250 g/9 oz potatoes	
250 g/9 oz carrots	
50 g/2 oz goose or pork drippings	
1 tbsp plain flour	
1 tsp salt	
Pinch freshly ground black pepper	
2 tbsp chopped fresh parsley	

Cut up goose carcass with poultry shears. Remove skin from meat. Cover carcass, skin and juices with the water and simmer for 30 minutes, covered. • Peel and chop onions. Peel, wash and chop turnips, potatoes and carrots. Cut up cooked goose meat. • Strain goose stock. • Heat dripping and fry onions until transparent; stir in flour and gradually add stock, stirring continously. Add turnips to sauce, cover and cook for 20 minutes. • Add chopped potatoes, carrots and salt and cook for 20 minutes longer. Add meat and heat with vegetables. Season stew with pepper and serve sprinkled with chopped parsley.

Cock-A-Leekie

A famous Scottish soup

Preparation time: 40 minutes
Cooking time: 1½ hours
Serves 4

1 large onion
1 small chicken weighing 1 kg/ 2¼ lbs with heart and liver
10 prunes
6 tbsp pearl barley
1 tsp salt
2 pinches freshly ground black pepper
800 g/1¾ lbs leeks
½ bunch parsley

Peel and chop onion. Wash chicken, put in pan with heart and prunes, barely cover with water and bring to the boil. Skim off scum as it forms. • Add chopped onion, barley, salt and pepper to chicken, cover and simmer very gently for 1½ hours so that the surface of the water barely moves. • Cut off green leaves from leeks, halve lengthwise, wash thoroughly, dry and slice. • Add leeks and liver to chicken after 1¼ hours and cook all together for last 15 minutes. • Remove cooked chicken from stock, skin it, take meat off bones and slice thinly. Slice heart and liver or discard as preferred. • In the meantime, continue to boil stock, uncovered, until reduced by one-third. • Return meat to stock and season well with salt and pepper. • Wash and dry parsley, remove stalks and chop leaves before sprinkling over soup.

Waterzooi

A Belgian speciality

Preparation time: 40 minutes
Cooking time: 1½ hours
Serves 4

200 g/7 oz brisket of beef
1.25 litres/2½ pt/5 cups water
2 tsp salt
6 allspice berries
6 black peppercorns
1 small chicken weighing 1.2 kg/2½ lbs
200 g/7 oz leeks
200 g/7 oz carrots
100g/4 oz celeriac
3 small onions
40g/1½ oz butter
2 tbsp plain flour
2 egg yolks
6 tbsp double (thick) cream
2 tsp lemon juice

Wash beef, bring to the boil with water, salt and spices, skimming off scum as it forms. Simmer gently for 45 minutes. • Cut chicken in half, rinse it with giblets, add to meat and cook for an additional 45 minutes. • Meanwhile, clean and wash leeks, scrape and rinse carrots, peel and rinse celeriac; cut into large pieces. Peel and halve onions, add to soup with other prepared vegetables. Cook vegetables for 30 minutes in soup. • Lift out beef and chicken and strain soup. Slice cooked carrots and leeks and chop celeriac, discard onion. • Melt butter, sweat flour in it, gradually add stock and simmer for a few minutes. • Remove chicken meat from carcass, cut up and return to soup with vegetables, putting beef and giblets aside to be used elsewhere. • Beat egg yolks with cream, thicken soup with this mixture and season to taste with salt and lemon juice.

Pasta and Chicken Stew

A Mediterranean speciality

Preparation time: 50 minutes
Cooking time: 1 hour, 35 minutes
Serves 4

1 roasting chicken weighing 1 kg/2¼ lbs	
1.5 litres/2½ pt/5 cups water	
1 tsp salt	
3 allspice berries	
3 black peppercorns	
1 bay leaf	
Soup vegetables, carrots, leek, celery, etc.	
2-3 small onions	
2 garlic cloves	
250 g/9 oz each aubergines, (eggplant) courgettes (zucchini) and small tomatoes	
Sprig thyme	
1 tbsp oil	
100 g/4 oz pasta bows	

Wash chicken and giblets, bring to the boil with water, salt, spices and bay leaf. Skim off scum as it forms. • Poach chicken 1½ hours in uncovered pan, allowing the surface of the liquid scarcely to move. • Wash, clean and chop soup vegetables, and add to chicken at the end of the first half hour. • Peel and chop onions and garlic. Wash, dry and chop aubergines (eggplant) and courgettes (zucchini). • Skin and chop tomatoes, removing core. Rinse thyme. • Heat oil; fry onions and garlic until transparent. Add chopped vegetables and thyme, continuing to fry for 10 minutes longer. • Strain chicken stock, adding 250 ml/8 fl oz/1 cup to vegetables. Bring remaining stock to the boil, add pasta and boil for 5 minutes. • Take chicken meat off carcass, cut up and add to vegetables. Pour cooked pasta and remaining stock over the mixture and combine.

Country Stew

Quick and easy

Preparation time: 1 hour
Cooking time: 45 minutes
Serves 4

800 g/1¾ lbs boned turkey thighs	
1 onion	
1 bay leaf	
2 cloves	
500–750 ml/¾–1¼ pts/2–3 cups water	
½ tsp salt	
2 carrots	
2 leeks	
125 ml/4 fl oz/½ cup double (thick) cream	
1 tbsp creamed horseradish	
2 tbsp grated fresh horseradish, optional	

Wash and dry meat. Peel onion and use the cloves to spike the bay leaf onto it. • Bring water to the boil. Add salt, onion and turkey; simmer for 45 minutes. Skim off any scum that forms during the first 20 minutes. • Scrape, wash and slice carrots thickly. Remove root end and dark green leaves from leeks, split in two lengthwise before washing thoroughly, and chop into 2 cm/¾ in pieces. • When turkey has been cooking for 20 minutes, add prepared vegetables and continue to cook in covered pan. • Whip cream lightly and stir in creamed horseradish. • Arrange meat and vegetables in a tureen, discarding onion and sprinkle with grated horseradish, if used. Serve horseradish cream separately. Good accompanied by rye bread.

Paella

A Spanish dish well worth the effort

Preparation and cooking time:
1 hour 15 minutes
Serves 6

| 1 chicken weighing 1 kg/2¼ lbs |
| 250 g/9 oz pork tenderloin |
| 1 tsp salt |
| 2 pinches freshly ground black pepper |
| 6 tbsp olive oil |
| 500 g/18 oz mussels |
| 6 king prawns |
| 300 g/11 oz/2 cups long grain-rice |
| 200 g/7 oz chorizos or similar highly seasoned smoked pork sausages |
| 2 small onions |
| 2 garlic cloves |
| 1 litre/1¾ pt/4 cups chicken stock |
| 125 ml/4 fl oz/½ cup dry white wine |
| 3 pinches saffron |
| 100 g/4 oz frozen peas |
| 4 tomatoes |
| 100 g/4 oz black olives |
| 1 lemon |

Wash chicken inside and out, dry and cut into 12 portions. Wash and dry pork fillet and cut into 2 cm/¾ in cubes. • Season chicken and pork with salt and pepper. • Heat 4 tbsp of the oil in a large skillet and brown chicken pieces thoroughly. Add cubed pork and brown it in the same way, then reduce heat and fry for 20 minutes longer, turning the meat frequently. • Wash and scrub mussels, removing beards. Peel prawns and make a shallow cut along centre back to remove veins. • Rinse rice several times until water runs clear, then drain. • Slice sausages and fry briefly with the meat. • Peel and finely chop onions and garlic, and brown in remaining oil in a large pan. Add rice, fry for a short time with onions before pouring in the stock and white wine. Stir in saffron. Boil rice gently on low heat for 10 minutes. • Add peas and cook 10 minutes longer. • Cut a shallow cross in rounded side of tomatoes, immerse in boiling water and remove skin. Cut in 8 pieces, taking out core. • Preheat oven to 200°C/400°F/Gas Mark 6. Spread the rice in the bottom of a paella pan or a large, flat ovenware dish. Arrange the pieces of chicken, pork and sausage, prepared mussels, prawns and tomato on the rice. Bring to the boil on the hob, cover with aluminium foil and place in preheated oven for 20-25 minutes. • Rinse olives under cold running water, dry and halve, removing stones. • Wash lemon in hot water, dry and cut in 8 segments. • Allow cooked paella to stand for 10 minutes in oven once it has been switched off, then scatter olives over the top, garnish with wedges of lemon and serve at once.

Variations: In Spain, paella is prepared in different ways according to region and what is available at the local market. In coastal areas, squid and various types of fish are used. Anyone who brings back genuine chorizos from a trip to Spain can prepare an authentic paella.

Southern Chicken Stew

A great dish from the southern States

Preparation time: 45 minutes
Cooking time: 1½ hours
Serves 4-6

1 small boiling chicken weighing 1.2 kg/2½ lbs
2 tsp salt
1 onion
3 medium potatoes
400 g/14 oz tomatoes
Small can kidney beans (200 g/7 oz)
Small can sweetcorn (200 g/7 oz)
Sugar
1 tsp salt
2 pinches white pepper
2 tbsp finely chopped chives

Wash chicken and cut into 8 pieces, then place in pan with giblets and boiling water just to cover. • Simmer on low heat without the lid for 45 minutes, removing scum as necessary. • Next add salt, cover pan with lid and cook chicken gently for 45 minutes more. • Peel onion and cut into rings. Scrub potatoes thoroughly under running warm water or peel, rinse and roughly chop. Add to chicken, together with onion for the final 20 minutes of cooking time. • Make crosswise cuts through the skin on the round side of tomatoes, plunge briefly into boiling water, then remove skin and core. Cut into segments. Add tomatoes, drained kidney beans and sweetcorn to chicken and cook together for last 10 minutes of cooking time. • Remove chicken from stew, separate meat from skin and bones, then cut into pieces and return to stew. Season with sugar, salt and pepper, then reheat. Sprinkle with chopped chives before serving.

Caucasian Chicken Stew

Economical Russian speciality

Preparation time: 30 minutes
Cooking time: 45 minutes
Serves 4

1 chicken weighing 1 kg/2¼ lbs
1 tsp salt
1 tsp paprika
Pinch freshly ground black pepper
4 tbsp oil
2 small onions
200 g/7 oz celeriac
1 carrot
150 g/5 oz cucumber
150 g/5 oz pumpkin (or courgettes, if unavailable)
100 g/4 oz/¾ cup long-grain rice
1 bay leaf
Pinch fennel seeds
1 litre/1¾ pt/4 cups water
1 pickled gherkin
4 tbsp soured cream

Wash and dry chicken, then quarter it. • Mix salt, paprika and pepper with 1 tbsp of the oil. Coat chicken pieces with this mixture and marinate for 10 minutes. • Peel onion and celeriac, scrape carrot, and rinse all three. Peel cucumber and pumpkin. Cut vegetables into 2.5 cm/1 in pieces. • Heat remaining oil in a large, flame-proof casserole. Sauté chicken, then add vegetables (except cucumber and pumpkin) and fry all together. • Wash rice, add it to chicken with bay leaf and fennel, pour on water, cover and cook gently on low heat for 30 minutes. • Preheat oven to 240°C/475°F/Gas Mark 9. • Add cubed cucumber and pumpkin to rice mixture. Place casserole, uncovered, in middle of oven and cook for 15 minutes. • Finely chop gerkhin and stir into soured cream. • Serve Caucasian Chicken Stew straight from the dish, with an island of cream floating in the middle.

Chicken in a Brick Pot

A favourite Italian dish

Preparation time: 25 minutes
Cooking time: 1½ hours
Serves 4

500 g/18 oz celery	
400 g/14 oz carrots	
400 g/14 oz small potatoes	
1 roasting chicken weighing 1.2 kg/2½ lbs	
1 tbsp lemon juice	
1 tsp salt	
½ tsp freshly ground white pepper	
50 g/2 oz thinly sliced bacon rashers	
5 tbsp dry white wine	
Sprig fresh rosemary	
2 sage leaves	
25 g/1 oz butter	

Soak brick pot and lid for about 20 minutes in cold water. • Wash celery, remove strings and cut into 2.5 cm/1 in lengths. Scrape, wash and dry carrots; cut into rounds. Peel and wash potatoes, then quarter them. • Cut chicken into 8 equal portions, wash these and dry before sprinkling with lemon juice. • Season with salt and pepper, rubbing in well. • Take brick out of water and line with bacon rashers. Arrange one half the vegetables in it, season lightly with salt and pepper. Lay chicken portions on top and finish with remaining vegetables, seasoning lightly again. • Sprinkle wine over vegetables. Wash and dry herbs before laying them on top. • Put lid on brick and place in bottom of cold oven. Turn oven to 220°C/425°F/Gas Mark 7. Bring up to heat and cook for 1 hour. • Remove lid 10 minutes before end of cooking time and dab small pieces of butter over vegetables.

Creamy Asparagus and Chicken Soup

Pricey but delicious

Preparation and cooking time:
1 hour
Serves 4

900g/2 lbs white asparagus	
2 litres/4 pt/8 cups water	
1 tsp salt	
500 g/18 oz boned chicken breast fillets, skinned	
1 tbsp clarified butter	
25g/1 oz butter	
2 heaped tbsp plain flour	
125 ml/4 fl oz/½ cup milk	
Good pinch each salt and white pepper	
1 egg yolk	
5 tbsp soured cream or yogurt	
2 tbsp chopped chives	

Peel ends of asparagus. Bring water and salt to the boil, add asparagus and boil for about 10 minutes, until cooked but still firm. • Wash and dry chicken fillets, cut into 2.5 cm/1 in cubes and sauté for 6 minutes in clarified butter. Remove cubes from pan. • Drain asparagus, putting aside 250 ml/8 fl oz/1 cup of the cooking water. • Melt butter in a skillet, sprinkle in flour, continue cooking until it turns slightly brown, then add milk gradually to form a creamy sauce. Season to taste with salt and pepper, then simmer gently, stirring continuously, for 10 minutes. • Cut asparagus into 4 cm/1½ in lengths and add to sauce with cubed chicken. • Whisk egg yolk with soured cream or yogurt, stir into sauce, remove from heat and sprinkle with chives.

Garbure Bearnaise

A speciality from France

Preparation time: 30 minutes
Cooking time: 1 hour, 50
minutes
Serves 4

2 goose leg pieces, weighing 600 g/1¼ lb each
1 litre/1¾ pt/4 cups water
1 tsp salt
1 onion
1 bay leaf
100 g/4 oz carrots
200 g/7 oz white turnips
200 g/7 oz potatoes
200 g/7 oz white cabbage
200 g/7 oz green beans
150 g/5 oz canned butter beans
2 sprigs chervil
Pinch white pepper
1 tbsp chopped parsley

Wash goose and bring to the boil with water and salt. Peel onion and add to pan with bay leaf. Cook for about 20 minutes, uncovered, removing scum as it forms. • Cover and simmer gently for 1 hour more. • Scrape or peel carrots and turnips before washing and chopping them. Peel potatoes and chop, not too finely. • Prepare cabbage, rinse leaves and shred. Wash and chop green beans. • Add all prepared vegetables, together with drained butterbeans, herbs and pepper to pan. Cover and simmer for 30 minutes. • Remove goose from pan and cut meat off bones, cut into cubes and return to pan. Sprinkle finished dish with parsley.

Soljanka

A Russian favourite

Preparation time: 30 minutes
Cooking time: 2 hours
Serves 4

1 small chicken weighing 1.2 kg/2½ lbs
Soup vegetables, carrots, leeks, celery, etc.
1 onion
1.5 litres/2½ pt/6 cups water
2 tsp salt
2 allspice berries
600 g/1¼ lb white cabbage
2 pickled gherkins
125 ml/4 fl oz/½ cup dry white wine
2 pinches white pepper
6 tbsp soured cream or yogurt
3 tbsp fresh dill

Wash chicken and giblets. • Clean and rinse soup vegetables, then coarsely chop. Peel and halve onion. • Bring water to the boil with salt and allspice berries. Put in chicken, onion and soup vegetables. Cook uncovered for 30 minutes, skimming off scum as it forms. Almost cover pan with lid and continue to cook chicken for 1 hour more. • Clean and rinse white cabbage and shred coarsely. Cut pickled gherkins into julienne strips, add both to pan and cover completely before continuing to cook. • Take chicken from pan, remove meat from carcass and cut into pieces. • Boil soup uncovered, until reduced by half. Return chicken meat to soup, add wine and season to taste with pepper. Stir soured cream or yogurt into soup. • Sprinkle with dill before serving.

Creole Jambalaya

A speciality from the U.S.A.

Preparation time: 45 minutes
Cooking time: 55 minutes
Serves 4

200 g/7 oz unsmoked gammon
1 chicken weighing 1.2 kg/2½ lbs
1 tsp salt
Pinch white pepper
5 tbsp oil
2-3 small onions
1 garlic clove
2 green and 1 red pepper
2 large tomatoes
750 ml/1¼ pt/3 cups hot chicken stock
250 g/9 oz/1⅔ cups long-grain rice
2 pinches cayenne pepper
2 pinches saffron
200 g/7 oz smoked garlic sausage
200 g/7 oz lean ham
200 g/7 oz cooked lobster

Wash and dry gammon and chicken, cutting gammon into 2 cm/¾ in pieces and chicken in 8 portions. • Mix salt and pepper and oil, pour over combined gammon and chicken, cover and leave to marinate for 30 minutes. • Peel and chop onions and garlic. Halve peppers, remove seeds, ribs and stems before rinsing, drying and chopping. Skin and chop tomatoes. • Brown meat in a large, heavy-bottomed pan. Add chopped onions, garlic and peppers, fry all together before pouring on half the stock. Cover and simmer for 30 minutes. • Add tomatoes, washed rice, remaining stock, cayenne pepper and saffron to meat, mixing in well, and continue to simmer for 20 minutes more. • Slice sausage, cut ham and lobster into strips. Lay on top of rice combination, heat through for 5 minutes.

Chicken Pot-Au-Feu

A cheap and classic French dish

Preparation time: 35 minutes
Cooking time: 1 hour
Serves 4

1 chicken weighing 1.2 kg/ 2½ lbs
750 ml/1¼ pt/3 cups chicken stock
100 g/4 oz carrots
200 g/7 oz leeks
2 small onions
500 g/18 oz sauerkraut
1 bay leaf
4 juniper berries
400 g/14 oz tomatoes
½ tsp each salt and freshly ground black pepper

Wash chicken, heart and liver, dry and divide chicken into 8 portions. • Bring chicken stock to the boil in a large flame-proof casserole. Place chicken portions and heart into stock, lower the heat and cook uncovered for 30 minutes. Skim off any scum that forms. • Scrape, rinse and chop carrots. Cut white part of leeks into 5 cm/2 in lengths, split these in half and wash. Peel onions and slice into rings. Roughly chop sauerkraut and combine with bay leaf and juniper berries. • Add all prepared vegetables and chicken liver to stock, cover and simmer for 30 minutes. • Make crosswise cuts in the rounded end of tomatoes, cover with boiling water, skin and cut into good-sized segments, removing any core. • Add prepared tomatoes 10 minutes before end of cooking time; season well with salt and pepper. • Serve with warm French bread.

Chicken Drumsticks with Lentils

A hearty stew

Preparation time: 25 minutes
Cooking time: 45 minutes
Serves 4

500 g/18 oz/3 cups lentils
1.5 litres/3 pt/6 cups water
250 ml/8 fl oz/1 cup dry red wine
4 chicken drumsticks weighing approx. 200 g/7 oz each
1 chicken stock cube
1 bay leaf
1 dried chilli
Pinch freshly ground white pepper
½ tsp dried thyme
1 tsp dried basil
100 g/4 oz streaky bacon
1 tbsp oil
2 onions
1 garlic clove
Pinch each sugar and salt
2 tbsp chopped fresh parsley

Wash lentils several times in a bowl of water, then cover with the water and red wine and bring to the boil. • Wash drumsticks and add to lentils together with crumbled stock cube. Add bay leaf, chilli, pepper, thyme and basil; bring to the boil again and simmer, covered, on gentle heat for 45 minutes. • Cut bacon into small squares and fry in oil. Peel onions and slice into rings before frying to a golden brown in bacon fat. Peel and crush garlic and mix with onions. • Season to taste with salt and sugar before serving sprinkled with chopped parsley and scattered with the onion mixture.

Turkey Liver Pilaff

Simple to make

Preparation time: 45 minutes
Cooking time: 50 minutes
Serves 4

250 g/9 oz/1⅔ cups long-grain rice
750 ml/1¼ pt/3 cups water
1 tsp salt
500 g/18 oz turkey livers
2-3 onions
2 red peppers
2 tbsp clarified butter
125 ml/4 fl oz/½ cup vegetable stock
4 tbsp white wine
Pinch each salt and white pepper
4 tbsp soured cream or yogurt
1 tbsp chopped fresh parsley

Wash rice in sieve under running water until it runs clear. • Bring water and salt to the boil, add rice, cover, turn heat low and leave to absorb liquid for about 20 minutes. • Wash and dry turkey livers, then cut into 2 cm/¾ in cubes. Peel and finely chop onions. Halve red peppers, remove stems, ribs and seeds before rinsing and chopping into fairly small pieces. • Heat 1 tbsp of the clarified butter in a heavy-bottomed pan, fry turkey livers for 4 minutes, then remove from pan and keep warm. • Put remaining clarified butter in pan with chopped onion and fry until transparent. Add chopped peppers and fry for 10 minutes longer. Pour in vegetable stock, cover and steam for 10 minutes. • Mix in rice, white wine and cooked liver. Season with salt and pepper, and stir in soured cream or yogurt and parsley.

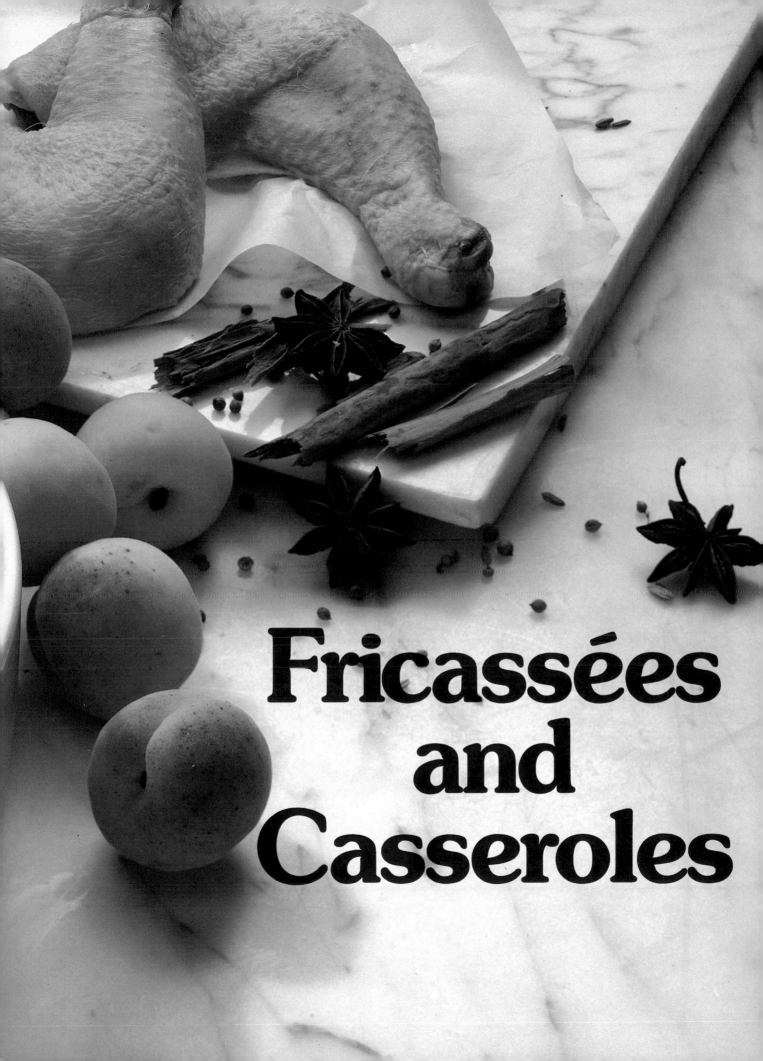

Fricassées and Casseroles

Braised Pigeons in Chocolate Sauce

An unusual Spanish dish

Preparation time: 40 minutes
Cooking time: 50 minutes
Serves 4

2 garlic cloves
4 pigeons weighing 500 g/18 oz each
1 tsp salt
2 pinches freshly ground black pepper
4 tbsp olive oil
1 tbsp plain flour
4 tbsp dry white wine
250 ml/8 fl oz/1 cup chicken stock
200 g/7 oz shallots
50 g/2 oz plain (dark) chocolate

Peel and finely chop the garlic. • Wash pigeons inside and out, then dry and rub with salt and pepper, inside and out. • Heat oil in large, heavy-bottomed pan and brown pigeons all over before removing from pan. Fry garlic in remaining oil. Stir flour into oil, fry briefly, then add wine and chicken stock. Simmer for 5 minutes, stirring constantly. • Put pigeons into sauce, cover and cook for 50 minutes on a low heat. • Peel shallots, chop finely and add to pigeons after 30 minutes. • Pre-heat oven to 120°C/225°F/Gas Mark ¼. • Arrange cooked pigeons on a serving dish and keep hot in oven. • Skim fat off sauce. Grate chocolate and add to sauce, stirring continuously over a low heat until melted. Do not let the sauce boil again. Season generously with salt and pepper and serve with pigeons. • To accompany this dish, serve either rice, cooked until just tender, or crisp French bread, and a fresh mixed salad.

Coq Au Vin

A French classic

Preparation time: 50 minutes
Cooking time: 50 minutes
Serves 6

1 chicken weighing 1.5 kg/3½ lbs
½ tsp salt
Pinch white pepper
100 g/4 oz bacon, in 1 piece
8 small onions
1 garlic clove
2 carrots
2 tbsp clarified butter
1 bay leaf
1 sprig thyme
2 sprigs parsley
750 ml/1¼ pt/3 cups dry red wine
150 g/5 oz button mushrooms
½ bunch flat-leaved parsley
1 tsp plain flour
2 tbsp brandy

Wash and dry chicken, cut into 8 portions and season with salt and pepper. Finely chop bacon, peel and chop onions and garlic. Clean, wash and chop carrots. • Heat clarified butter in a heavy-bottomed pan and brown chicken pieces and bacon. Add chopped onion and garlic with rest of prepared vegetables and continue to fry. • Add bay leaf, thyme and parsley sprigs with red wine. Cook chicken for 40 minutes. • Clean, wash and chop mushrooms. • Remove chicken from pan and keep warm. Rub vegetables with cooking juices through a sieve, then simmer mushrooms in this sauce for 10 minutes. • Wash and chop parsley. • Thicken sauce with flour mixed to a paste with cold water. Season with salt and brandy, then pour over chicken. Bring to the boil and cook for 1 minute. Sprinkle with parsley.

Coq Au Riesling

A speciality from Alsace

Preparation time: 30 minutes
Cooking time: 35 minutes
Serves 4–6

1 chicken weighing 1.5 kg/ 3½ lbs
150 g/5 oz shallots
1 tsp salt
2 garlic cloves
½ bunch fresh tarragon
75 g/3 oz butter
½ tsp white pepper
2 tbsp chopped parsley
500 ml/16 fl oz/2 cups Alsatian Riesling (white wine)
200 g/7 oz button mushrooms
½ tsp plain flour
200ml/7 fl oz/¾ cup soured cream

Cut wings off chicken. Peel and quarter shallots. Put 1 shallot, together with wings, some salt and 250 ml/8 fl oz/1 cup water, in a pan and simmer for 20 minutes. Strain stock. • Wash and dry remaining chicken, then cut in 8 pieces. • Peel and chop garlic. Rinse and finely chop tarragon, reserving some leaves for garnish. • Melt half the butter and brown chicken pieces. Add pepper, salt, shallots, garlic, herbs, wine and stock. Cover and cook for 25 minutes. • Rinse mushrooms, slice thinly, sprinkle with flour and brown in remaining butter. • Remove lid from pan, increase heat and continue to cook chicken for another 10 minutes until done. • Lift out chicken pieces and keep warm. • Stir soured cream into sauce together with mushrooms. Season to taste with salt and pepper and pour over chicken. Garnish with tarragon.

Pigeons with Bulgar Wheat Stuffing

An Egyptian speciality

Preparation time: 25 minutes
Cooking time: 30 minutes
Serves 4

4 young pigeons weighing 250 g/9 oz each
1 bunch spring onions
65 g/2½ oz butter
100 g/4 oz/⅔ cup bulgar wheat
½ tbsp freshly chopped mint
1 tsp salt
½ tsp freshly ground black pepper
750 ml/24 fl oz/3 cups chicken stock

Wash and dry pigeons and giblets. Finely chop giblets.
• Clean, rinse and chop spring onions, combine with giblets and brown in 1 tbsp of the butter. Add bulgar wheat and chopped mint. Season stuffing with salt and pepper. • Rub insides of pigeons with salt and fill each with 2 tbsp of wheat mixture. Sew cavity openings together. • Preheat oven to 220°C/425°F/Gas Mark 7. • Put pigeons in roasting pan. Melt remaining butter and trickle over pigeons. Pour 500 ml/16 fl oz/2 cups of the chicken stock into a pan and bring to the boil on the hotplate. • Roast pigeons for 30 minutes in oven, basting frequently with liquid. • Meanwhile, bring remaining stock to the boil, add rest of bulgar wheat mixture to it and simmer over low heat for 30 minutes to allow wheat to absorb liquid. Spoon onto a warm serving dish and arrange pigeons on top.

Braised Quails

A speciality from Lebanon

Preparation time: 20 minutes
Cooking time: 1½ hours
Serves 4

8 quails weighing 100 g/4 oz each
1 tsp salt
½ tsp white pepper
8 thin rashers streaky bacon (100 g/4 oz)
4 tbsp oil
50 g/2 oz/⅓ cup sultanas
2 small onions
4 allspice berries
100 ml/3 fl oz/⅓ cup sweet white wine (Sauterne)
1 clove garlic
200 g/7 oz/1⅓ cups long-grain rice
750 ml/24 fl oz/3 cups chicken stock
2 pinches saffron

Wash and dry quails and season with salt and pepper. Wrap a rasher of bacon round each and tie securely with kitchen thread. • Heat 2 tbsp of the oil in a heavy-bottomed pan, brown quails for 10 minutes then take them out and keep warm. • Wash and drain sultanas. • Peel and chop onions; brown two-thirds of them in oil left in the pan. Add sultanas, allspice berries and white wine with an equal quantity of water to pan, bring to the boil and season to taste with salt. Simmer sauce gently for 20 minutes on low heat, then strain. • Cook quails for 20 minutes in sauce. • Peel and chop garlic, then fry in a separate pan with remaining onion in 2 tbsp oil. Add washed rice, chicken stock and saffron to pan and cook all together for 20 minutes. • Serve quails over the rice with the sauce passed separately.

Turkey and Curd Cheese Roulades

Easier than you'd think

Preparation time: 30 minutes
Cooking time: 20 minutes
Serves 4

2 medium carrots
1 small onion
3 tbsp clarified butter
2 tbsp chopped mixed herbs (e.g. dill, chervil, thyme, parsley, lemon balm)
100 g/4 oz curd cheese
1 egg yolk
1 tbsp mustard
Pinch each salt and freshly ground white pepper
4 turkey escalopes (sliced thin) weighing 175 g/6 oz each
250 ml/8 fl oz/1 cup hot chicken stock
4 tbsp dry vermouth
2 tbsp soured cream

Peel and rinse carrots before cutting into julienne strips. Peel and chop onion. • Heat 1 tbsp of the clarified butter. Sweat prepared onion and carrots over low heat for 5 minutes, then cool slightly. • Mix herbs with curd cheese, egg yolk, mustard, salt and pepper. • Wash and dry turkey escalopes, then spread with herb and cheese mixture. Divide cooled vegetables into 4 portions and arrange on top of cheese. Roll meat up and fasten with cocktail sticks. • Heat remaining clarified butter and brown roulades thoroughly over moderate heat. Add chicken stock and vermouth; cover and simmer for 20 minutes over low heat until done. • Stir soured cream into cooking juices. Serve with parsley potatoes.

Turkey and Vegetable Roulades

Quick and easy

Preparation time: 45 minutes
Cooking time: 45 minutes
Serves 4

50 g/2 oz/⅓ cup sultanas
100 g/4 oz ham
1 bunch parsley
2 tbsp pine kernels
1 tbsp capers
4 turkey escalopes (sliced thin) weighing 175 g/6 oz each
4 pinches each salt and white pepper
1 small onion
4 tbsp olive oil
1 can tomato purée (paste) (70 g/2½ oz)
125 ml/4 fl oz/½ cup water
250 ml/8 fl oz/1 cup single (light) cream
1 small bay leaf
3 rosemary leaves
Pinch dried thyme
1 red pepper
Pinch sugar

Cover sultanas with water and bring to the boil. • Cube ham. Wash, dry and chop parsley. • Drain sultanas; mix with ham, parsley, pine kernels and capers. • Wash and dry turkey escalopes, sprinkle with salt and pepper. Spread meat with filling, roll up and fasten with cocktail sticks. • Peel and chop onion. • Heat oil. Brown roulades thoroughly, then add chopped onions and fry briefly with meat. Add tomato purée (paste) with water, cream, bay leaf and other herbs. Cover and simmer roulades for 20 minutes. • Clean, wash and dry red pepper, cut into strips and cook for last 10 minutes with meat. Season sauce with sugar to taste.

Hungarian Turkey Ragoût

Quick and easy to prepare

Preparation and cooking time: 30 minutes
Serves 4

500 g/18 oz turkey breast
2 onions
250 g/9 oz button mushrooms
1 tbsp lemon juice
2 tbsp oil
25 g/1 oz butter
125 ml/4 fl oz/½ cup soured cream
2 tsp cornflour
1 tsp paprika
125 ml/4 fl oz/½ cup dry white wine
½ tsp each salt and white pepper

Wash and dry meat before cutting into thin slices. • Peel and finely chop onions. Wash and trim mushrooms, slice thinly and sprinkle with lemon juice. • Heat oil in a large, heavy-bottomed pan. Brown meat, turning until done, then remove from pan. • Melt butter with oil in the pan and fry onions until transparent. Add mushrooms, cover and sweat for 10 minutes. • Mix soured cream with cornflour and paprika. • Return meat to pan with mushrooms, add cream mixture and then white wine. Simmer ragoût gently for a few minutes. • Season to taste with salt and pepper. • Potato croquettes or noodles and a fresh green salad go well with this dish.

Turkey Liver with Banana Rice

Quick and easy

Preparation time: 35 minutes
Cooking time: 20 minutes
Serves 4

200 g/7 oz/1⅓ cups long-grain rice
2.5 litres/5 pt/10 cups water
1 tsp salt
600 g/1¼ lbs turkey liver
1 tbsp plain flour
100 g/4 oz shallots
65g/2½ oz butter
3 tbsp curry powder
50 g/2 oz slivered almonds
125 ml/4 fl oz/½ cup single (light) cream
125 ml/4 fl oz/½ cup chicken stock
2 pinches white pepper
2 small bananas
1 tsp lemon juice

Wash rice in sieve under running water until water runs clear. • Bring water and salt to the boil. Turn rice into rapidly-boiling water and continue to boil for 20 minutes. • Wash liver carefully and dry, cut evenly into slices and dust with flour. • Peel and finely chop shallots. • Melt 40 g/1½ oz of the butter in a large, heavy-bottomed pan and fry shallots until transparent. Add liver and continue to fry for 5 minutes, turning continuously. Sprinkle 2 tbsp of the curry powder and the slivered almonds over liver. Add cream and chicken stock, then simmer very gently over low heat for 5 minutes. Season to taste with salt and pepper. • Drain rice in a sieve. • Peel and slice bananas before browning in remaining butter. Mix remaining curry powder and rice with banana slices, adding lemon juice to taste. • Serve ragoût with banana rice.

Chicken Liver and Lentils

Economical, quick and easy

Preparation time: 40 minutes
Cooking time: 20 minutes
Serves 4

1 litre/1¾ pt/4 cups water
350 g/12 oz/2 cups red lentils
100 g/4 oz ham without fat
500 g/18 oz chicken livers
1 bunch parsley
½ bunch sage
75 g/3 oz butter
1 tbsp olive oil
3 tbsp chicken stock
1 tsp salt
2 pinches black pepper

Bring water to the boil and cook lentils over low heat for 8 minutes, then drain in sieve. • Finely chop ham. Wash livers in cold water, dry, remove any fat or skin and cut into strips. • Wash, dry and finely chop parsley and sage. • Melt half the butter with oil in a large pan. Fry ham and herbs over low heat, stirring, then add chicken stock. Cover and continue to cook for 5 minutes longer. • Melt remaining butter, fry chicken livers for 3–4 minutes, turning constantly. Season with salt and pepper, mix with lentils and serve immediately. • Mashed potatoes or hot French bread should accompany this dish.

Tip: Chicken livers may be combined with sweetcorn or peas instead of the lentils used here.

Chicken Liver in Yogurt Sauce

Quick and good value

Preparation and cooking time: 35 minutes
Serves 6

1 bunch each parsley, basil and chives
300 ml/½ pt/½ cup thick-set yogurt
4 tbsp single (light) cream
1 tsp lemon juice
1 garlic clove
Pinch each salt, white pepper and sugar
500 g/18 oz chicken livers
2 small onions
3 tbsp oil
1 tbsp plain flour
½ tsp dried mixed herbs
Pinch salt
2 pinches freshly ground black pepper

Wash and dry herbs and chop finely. Mix yogurt with cream, lemon juice and herbs. • Peel and chop garlic, sprinkle with salt and crush before adding to yogurt mixture. Season to taste with pepper and sugar. Set aside. • Remove any fat or skin from chicken livers, wash and dry. • Peel onions and cut into thin rings. • Heat 1 tbsp of the oil in a pan, brown onion rings for about 5 minutes, then remove from pan. • Heat remaining oil in pan. Roll liver in flour and fry in small amounts for about 2 minutes until brown. Sprinkle with dried herbs. Finally, add fried onions to liver, continue to fry for 1 minute longer, season to taste with salt and pepper before serving with yogurt sauce. • Potatoes boiled in their skins are tasty with this dish.

Chicken Livers with Vegetables

Simple and tasty

Preparation time: 1 hour
Cooking time: 20 minutes
Serves 6

1 kg/2¼ lbs chicken livers
2 small onions
2 stalks celery
250 g/9 oz each small carrots, shallots and potatoes
4 tbsp olive oil
125 ml/4 fl oz/½ cup dry white wine
250 ml/8 fl oz/1 cup chicken stock
2 pinches salt
Pinch freshly ground black pepper
1 bunch parsley

Slice livers in half, cutting off any tissue. Rinse thoroughly and pat dry. • Peel and roughly chop onions. Remove coarse strings from celery, wash and slice thinly. Scrape carrots, wash and cut into rounds. Peel and chop shallots and potatoes. • Heat 3 tbsp of the oil in a heavy-bottomed pan. Fry onions until transparent, then add livers and continue to fry until they turn light grey. Remove livers and set aside. Pour in white wine and allow to evaporate while stirring continuously. • Stir in vegetables and chicken stock, season to taste with salt and pepper. Cook gently on low heat until vegetables are tender, about 15 minutes. • Return livers to pan with remaining oil. Wash, dry and chop parsley, then sprinkle over the finished dish.

Turkey Liver and Tomato

A quick and economical dish

Preparation time: 40 minutes
Cooking time: 20 minutes
Serves 4

2 large onions
3 ripe tomatoes
75g/3 oz butter
100 ml/3 fl oz/⅓ cup dry white wine
500 g/18 oz turkey livers
1 tsp plain flour
½ tsp salt
2 sprigs sage
2 pinches freshly ground black pepper

Peel onions and slice into rings. Cut a shallow cross in rounded end of tomatoes, immerse briefly in boiling water, then skin and cut into segments, removing core. • Melt half the butter in a pan, brown onions, pour in white wine and cover, then simmer for about 5 minutes until done. • Add tomato segments to onions, cook over medium heat 5 minutes longer, uncovered, to thicken liquid slightly. • Wash and pat dry turkey livers, removing any fat or skin. Cut into strips and dust with flour. • Wash and dry sage. • Heat remaining butter in another pan and fry liver strips until they turn grey. • Add cooked liver to tomato sauce, seasoning with salt and pepper, and sprinkling with sage leaves. Serve hot, preferably with parsley potatoes.

Tip: Cooked rice may be added to the finished dish, provided some chicken broth has been added to the sauce.

Poultry Liver with Celery

Simple to prepare

Preparation and cooking time: 1 hour
Serves 4

800 g/1¾ lbs poultry liver
1 tbsp plain flour
3 tbsp olive oil
2 small onions
1 can chopped tomatoes (400 g/14 oz)
2 large tomatoes
1 head of celery
½ tsp salt
Pinch white pepper
1 tsp dried oregano
100 g/4 oz/1 cup walnut pieces
125 ml/4 fl oz/½ cup soured cream
½ bunch lemon balm

Wash and pat dry livers, remove any skin or fat and cut into pieces. • Dust livers with flour, brown well on all sides in olive oil and remove from pan. • Peel and finely chop onions before frying until transparent in remaining oil. • Drain tomatoes, rub through sieve and add purée to onions. Simmer to allow sauce to thicken slightly. • Make a shallow cross in tomato skins, cover with boiling water, skin and cut into segments, removing hard core. • Pull off celery string, then wash stalks and chop in 2 cm/¾ in pieces. Add prepared tomatoes and celery to tomato purée. Cover and simmer for 15 minutes, then season with salt, pepper and oregano. • Wash and dry lemon balm leaves. Chop walnuts and add to vegetables with livers and soured cream. Reheat fricassee, then sprinkle with lemon balm. • Serve with mashed potatoes.

Chicken Curry

A family favourite

Total preparation time: 30 minutes
Serves 3-4

500 g/18 oz chicken breast fillets
½ bunch spring onions
1 large tomato
½ pineapple (approx. 500 g/18 oz)
2 tbsp clarified butter
1 tsp plain flour
2 tbsp curry powder
250 ml/8 fl oz/1 cup chicken stock
1 tsp lemon juice
Pinch salt

Wash and dry meat and cut into 1 cm/⅓ in wide strips. • Chop dark green ends off spring onions; wash and dry, then chop light green parts into 1 cm/⅓ in rings. Slice white ends in quarters lengthwise. • Cover tomato with boiling water, skin and chop. • Divide pineapple into 8, cut away hard core, loosen flesh from skin and cut across in thin slices. • Heat clarified butter and brown chicken. Add onions and chopped tomato; fry 1 minute longer. • Combine flour and curry powder, then stir into fricassee. Add chicken stock slowly, stirring well. • Add pineapple pieces and heat gently for 5 minutes. Season curry to taste with lemon juice and salt. • Serve with rice cooked until just tender.

Fricassée with Walnuts

Quick and easy

Preparation and cooking time: 35 minutes
Serves 3–4

500 g/18 oz chicken breast fillets
3 tbsp soy sauce
2 tbsp dry sherry
½ tsp sugar
Pinch salt
2 tbsp cornflour
1 red pepper
2 small onions
2-3 celery stalks
5 tbsp oil
100 g/4 oz/1 cup walnut halves
125 ml/4 fl oz/½ cup hot chicken stock

Wash and dry meat; cut into 2 cm/¾ in cubes. • Mix soy sauce, sherry, sugar, salt and cornflour together and combine with meat. • Remove stem, ribs and seeds from red pepper; wash and dry, then cut into strips. Peel and halve onions; cut into strips. String celery, wash and dry, then cut into julienne strips. • Heat 1 tbsp oil and brown walnut halves, then remove from pan. • Add 1 tbsp oil to pan and brown first celery, then onions and pepper, one minute each over high heat. Take vegetables out of pan. • Heat remaining oil in pan, fry chicken cubes for 3 minutes, turning frequently. Turn heat down and pour on chicken stock. Heat vegetables and walnuts briefly in fricassee. Serve with rice.

Chicken Fricassée

A dinner party dish

Preparation time: 30 minutes
Cooking time: 1 hour
Serves 4

1 chicken weighing
1.5 kg/3½ lbs

1 bay leaf

2 small onions

1 tsp each salt and peppercorns

Pinch white pepper

Soup vegetables, carrots, leek, celery, etc.

50 g/2 oz butter

125 ml/4 fl oz/½ cup dry white wine

250 ml/8 fl oz/1 cup single (light) cream

125 g/4 fl oz/½ cup soured cream

200 g/7 oz carrots

150 g/5 oz celeriac

1 small turnip

1 small leek

½ tsp dried tarragon

1 tbsp chopped parsley

Remove legs and breast from chicken. Cut rest of bird into several pieces, put in pot with bay leaf, 1 washed but unpeeled onion, salt, peppercorns and about 1 litre/1¾ pt/4 cups water. Bring to the boil and cook uncovered for 30 minutes, until liquid is reduced to about 250 ml/8 fl oz/1 cup. • Strain chicken stock. Keep cooked meat to use elsewhere. • Wash, dry and halve chicken breasts and legs, then rub pepper in well. • Wash and finely chop soup vegetables. Peel second onion and chop. • Brown chicken pieces in butter, add prepared soup vegetables and onion and continue to fry. Pour in chicken stock and wine, then cook for 30 minutes until meat is done. The stock should boil down to half its

original quantity. • Mix in creams and again reduce by half. • Peel or scrape carrots, celeriac, turnip and leek. Cut in julienne strips and stir into sauce with tarragon and parsley. Simmer gently for 3 minutes.

Chicken Fricassée with Millet

Healthy and economical

Preparation time: 30 minutes
Cooking time: 1 hour
Serves 4

1 chicken weighing 1 kg/2¼ lbs

1 tsp sea salt

1 small bay leaf

5 white peppercorns

1 vegetable stock cube

1 carrot

200 g/7 oz/1 cup millet

500 g/18 oz leek

50g/2 oz butter

125 ml/4 fl oz/½ cup single (light) cream

2 tbsp chopped fresh parsley

Juice of ½ lemon

Pinch each salt and freshly ground white pepper

Wash chicken, put in pot with salt, bay leaf, peppercorns and stock cube. Cover with water and cook for 1 hour until tender. • Strain stock and measure 750 ml/24 fl oz/3 cups, keeping the rest for later use. • Scrape, wash and chop carrot. Add with millet to stock, cover and cook for 30 minutes over low heat until soft. • Halve and wash leeks; cut into strips and cook for 10 minutes in butter. • Take meat off bone, cut into 5 cm/2 in pieces and combine with millet, leek, cream and parsley. Season with lemon juice, salt and pepper.

Chicken Marengo

A popular classic dish

Total preparation time: 1 hour
Serves 4

1 chicken weighing 1.2 kg/2½ lbs
½ tsp white pepper
125 ml/4 fl oz/½ cup olive oil
200 g/7 oz button mushrooms
Juice of 1 lemon
250 ml/8 fl oz/1 cup chicken stock
6 anchovy fillets
2 garlic cloves
Sprig parsley
2 sprigs thyme
1 bay leaf
400 g/14 oz tomatoes
12 black olives
2 boiled eggs

Wash chicken and giblets. Cut chicken into 8 serving pieces, pat dry and rub well with pepper and a small amount of olive oil. • Clean and wash mushrooms, slice and sprinkle with lemon juice. • Heat chicken stock. Chop anchovies finely. Peel and chop garlic. Wash and dry herbs; tie in bunch with bay leaf. • Brown chicken pieces thoroughly in remaining oil for 10 minutes. Add mushrooms, anchovies, garlic, herbs and hot chicken stock; cover and simmer all together over medium heat for 25 minutes. • Skin and coarsely chop tomatoes, removing cores. Add tomatoes and olives to chicken for final 5 minutes of cooking time. • Peel and finely chop boiled eggs. Sprinkle over dish just before serving.

Braised Paprika Chicken

Economical speciality from Hungary

Total preparition time: 50 minutes
Serves 4

| 1 chicken weighing |
| 1.2 kg/2½ lbs |
| 2 small onions |
| 2 each red and green peppers |
| 3 tbsp clarified butter |
| 6 tbsp chicken stock |
| 125 ml/4 fl oz/½ cup soured cream |
| 1 tbsp paprika |
| 1 tsp salt |
| Pinch white pepper |
| 1 tbsp finely chopped parsley |

Wash chicken (and any giblets there may be) thoroughly both inside and out, dry well and divide into 8 serving pieces. • Peel and finely chop onions. Halve peppers, remove stems, ribs and seeds, wash in lukewarm water. Then dry and cut into 3 cm/1 ¼ in wide strips. • Heat clarified butter in a large, heavy-bottomed pan and fry onions until transparent, turning continuously. • Add chicken pieces and continue to fry for a few minutes, while turning. Add prepared peppers and chicken stock, cover and cook gently over low heat for 30 minutes. • Meanwhile, stir soured cream, paprika, salt and pepper together; add to chicken at the end of 30 minutes. Allow to stand for 5 minutes. Sprinkle parsley over chicken before serving. • Tender boiled rice goes well with this dish.

Chicken Béarnaise

Classic French recipe

Preparation time: 40 minutes
Cooking time: 1½ hours
Serves 4

| 1 chicken weighing |
| 1.2 kg/2½ lbs |
| 1 dry bread roll |
| 150 g/5 oz lean boiled ham, |
| 1 garlic clove |
| 200 g/7 oz sausagemeat |
| 2 tbsp chopped chives |
| 1 litre/1¾ pt/4 cups water |
| 1 tsp salt |
| Sprig fresh thyme |
| 2 sprigs flat-leaved parsley |
| 1 bay leaf |
| 2 small onions |
| 2 small carrots |
| 1 small piece celeriac |
| 2 small leeks |
| 400 g/14 oz Savoy cabbage |
| 200 g/7 oz French beans |

Wash and dry chicken and giblets. • Soak bread roll in cold water. • Chop ham and giblets. Peel and chop garlic, and combine with ham, giblets, sausagemeat, chives and crumbled bread roll. • Fill chicken with stuffing, fastening opening together with cocktail sticks. • Bring water to the boil with salt, herbs and bay leaf. Put in chicken and cook, covered, for 1 hour. • Peel and chop onions. Clean or scrape carrots, celeriac and leeks, then wash and chop them. Cut cabbage in fine strips. Clean and wash beans, then break into pieces. Add prepared vegetables to chicken and cook all together for an additional 30 minutes.

Braised Rosemary Chicken

Quick and easy

Preparation and cooking time: 1 hour
Serves 4

1 roasting chicken weighing 1.2 kg/2½ lbs
1 tsp salt
2 tbsp clarified butter
125 ml/4 fl oz/½ cup hot chicken stock
1 sprig rosemary
1 small cooking apple
1 small floury potato
125 ml/4 fl oz/½ cup dry white wine
Pinch each salt and white pepper

Wash chicken and giblets thoroughly, then dry them. Cut chicken into 8 serving portions and rub well with salt. • Melt clarified butter in heavy-bottomed pot and brown chicken pieces on all sides. Add chicken stock and rosemary, together with heart and gizzard, cover and simmer on low heat for 30 minutes. • Meanwhile, chop liver finely. Peel apple. Peel potato under running water, rinse and grate with apple. Add grated apple and potato, liver and white wine to chicken, with a little more stock if necessary. • Continue to braise chicken for 10 more minutes, seasoning to taste with salt and pepper. • Serve with noodles.

Chicken Drumsticks in a Roasting Bag

Economical and easy to prepare

Preparation time: 20 minutes
Cooking time: 35 minutes
Serves 4

4 chicken drumsticks weighing 200 g/7 oz each
1 tsp salt
1 tbsp paprika
2 tbsp clarified butter
2 shallots
200 g/7 oz leeks, white part only
¼ cauliflower
2 red peppers
125 ml/4 fl oz/½ cup chicken stock
2 tbsp medium sherry
2 tbsp chopped chives

Wash and dry drumsticks, rub well with salt and paprika, then brown thoroughly in clarified butter over low heat. • Preheat oven to 220°C/425°F/Gas Mark 7, removing wire shelf. • Peel shallots and cut into eighths. Clean and halve leeks, wash and cut into 3 cm/1¼ in pieces. • Divide cauliflower in florets, wash thoroughly and leave to drain. • Cut peppers in half, remove stem, ribs and seeds, wash and chop into good-sized pieces. • Lift drumsticks out of fat and place in roasting bag with prepared vegetables and chicken stock. Seal bag well, piercing upper surface several times with a needle, and place bag in roasting pan. • Slide into middle of oven and cook for 35 minutes. • Transfer drumsticks and vegetables with cooking juices to a serving dish. • Sprinkle with sherry and chives. • Serve with plain boiled potatoes.

Chicken Pie

A family favourite

Preparation time: 1½ hours
Baking time: 25 minutes
Serves 4

1 chicken weighing 1 kg/2¼ lbs

1 litre/1¾ pt/4 cups water

1 tsp sea salt

250 g/9 oz/2¼ cups wholewheat flour

1 tsp baking powder

Pinch each sea salt, curry powder and freshly ground black pepper

175 g/6 oz softened butter

1 egg

2 small onions

1 carrot

100 g/4 oz button mushrooms

1 tbsp chopped parsley

1 tsp chopped basil

½ tsp each sea salt and freshly ground black pepper

Pinch cayenne pepper

For the pie dish: butter

For the glaze: 1 egg yolk

Wash chicken, cover with salted water and cook for 1 hour. • Mix 200 g/7 oz/1¾ cups flour with baking powder, curry powder and pepper, then knead to a dough with butter and egg. Put to one side to rest. • Peel and finely chop onions, then fry until transparent in remaining butter. • Scrape carrot, or trim and peel it with mushrooms, then chop all finely. Fry for 5 minutes with onions. • Lift chicken out of stock, take meat off bone and cut into 2 cm/¾ in pieces. Measure out 250 ml/8 fl oz/1 cup stock, putting rest aside to use elsewhere. • Whisk remaining flour into the stock and add to vegetables, allowing all to simmer for 5 minutes longer. Add meat, herbs and seasoning. • Pre-heat oven to 200°C/400°F/Gas Mark 6. Grease pie dish and pour in meat filling. • Roll dough out somewhat bigger than dish, lay filling on top and press edges down firmly onto dish. Prick lid well and brush with egg yolk. • Bake for 25 minutes until well browned.

Creamed Chicken

Takes time but is well worth the effort

Preparation time: 30 minutes
Cooking time: 1½ hours
Serves 4

1 chicken weighing 1.2 k/2½ lbs
1.5 litres/2½ pt/6 cups water
2 tsp salt
1 large carrot
2 small onions
2 leeks
⅛ celeriac
250 ml/8 fl oz/1 cup single (light) cream
1 tbsp medium dry sherry
1–2 pinches salt
1–2 tsp curry powder
1 tsp lemon juice
4 slices white bread weighing 50 g/2 oz each
75 g/3 oz butter

Wash chicken and giblets. Bring water and salt to the boil, then add chicken. Keep skimming off any scum that forms during first 20 minutes. • Scrape and rinse carrot; cut into pieces. Peel onions and cut into 8 pieces. Wash leeks and celeriac before chopping roughly. Add prepared vegetables to chicken and reduce heat until stock barely simmers. Poach chicken gently, uncovered, for 1 hour longer. • Lift chicken from stock, remove skin, take meat off the bone and cut into even pieces. Place in small frying pan. • Add cream and reduce slightly. Season with sherry, salt, curry powder and lemon juice, thinning with a few tablespoons of chicken stock if necessary. • Fry slices of bread in foaming butter until brown on both sides; divide among 4 plates and spoon over chicken fricassee. • Serve immediately.

Chicken à la King

Quick and tasty

Preparation and cooking time: 35 minutes
Serves 4

200 g/7 oz button mushrooms
600 g/1¼ lbs chicken breast fillets
1 red pepper
40 g/1½ oz butter
125 ml/4 fl oz/½ cup single (light) cream
2 tbsp plain flour
125 ml/4 fl oz/½ cup chicken stock
1 tsp seasoning salt
Pinch freshly ground black pepper
Juice of 1 lemon
1 tbsp chopped parsley

Wash, and trim button mushrooms. • Wash chicken, remove any skin or bones and cut in 1 cm/½ in wide strips. • Halve pepper, remove stalk, ribs and seeds, then blanch 5 minutes in boiling salted water, drain and chop finely. • Melt butter. Fry mushrooms and chicken strips for 5 minutes, turning frequently. • Whisk cream with flour and stock, before adding to chicken. Add chopped pepper. Simmer gently for 5 minutes, adding a little more stock if necessary to form a creamy sauce. • Remove pan from heat, season to taste with seasoning salt, pepper and lemon juice, then sprinkle with parsley.

Circassian Chicken

A speciality from Russia

Preparation time: 40 minutes
Cooking time: 1½ hours
Serves 4

1 chicken weighing 1.2 kg/2½ lbs	
1 tsp salt	
Soup vegetables, carrots, leek, celery, etc.	
2 onions	
1 bay leaf	
1 clove	
½ dry bread roll	
150 g/5 oz/1¼ cups shelled walnuts	
2 tsp oil	
1 tsp salt	
1 tbsp chopped parsley	
2 tbsp soured cream	

Wash chicken and giblets, add salt, cover with boiling water and bring back to the boil. Remove any scum that forms during first 30 minutes. • Poach chicken for 30 minutes on such a low heat that cooking liquid barely moves. • Wash, clean and chop soup vegetables. Peel and quarter one onion, then spike bay leaf to one quarter with clove. • After 30 minutes add prepared vegetables to chicken and continue to simmer for 1 hour longer until chicken is done. • Soak roll in cold water. • Peel second onion and chop finely. Grind two-thirds of nuts and coarsely chop the rest. • Heat oil and fry onion until golden brown, then add ground nuts and fry briefly. • Crumble the roll and mix to a smooth paste with fried onion and nuts, salt, parsley, chopped nuts and soured cream. • Remove chicken from stock, take meat off the bone and cut into pieces, then keep warm. •

Strain stock and reduce slightly by boiling uncovered. • Stir 250 ml/8 fl oz stock into nut mixture, then add meat to sauce. • Serve with fluffy boiled rice.

Turkey Fricassee

Quick and easy

Preparation and cooking time: 25 minutes
Serves 6

1 kg/2¼ lbs turkey steak	
1 tbsp flour	
2 small onions	
2 tbsp oil	
125 ml/4 fl oz/½ cup chicken stock	
Bunch mixed herbs (chervil, tarragon, parsley)	
1 tsp curry powder	
150 ml/5 fl oz/⅔ cup soured cream	
1 tbsp small capers	

2 pinches each salt and freshly ground white pepper

Wash and pat dry meat, then cut into fine strips and coat in flour. • Peel onions and chop finely. • Heat oil in large pan. Brown meat quickly over high heat, turning frequently. Add onions and continue to fry, then gradually add stock. Simmer together for 5 minutes. • Wash and dry herbs before chopping finely. • Stir curry powder into soured cream and add to chicken mixture with capers and herbs. Season with salt and pepper. • Serve with buttered noodles and a mixed salad.

Basque Chicken

A great Spanish dish

Preparation time: 1 hour
Cooking time: 1 hour
Serves 4

1 chicken weighing 1 kg/2¼ lbs
800 g/1¾ lbs tomatoes
2 green peppers
2 onions
3 garlic cloves
5 tbsp olive oil
125 ml/4 fl oz/½ cup hot chicken stock
1½ tsp salt
2 pinches freshly ground black pepper
250 g/9 oz/1⅔ cups long-grain rice
1 tbsp paprika

Wash and dry chicken and giblets. Cut chicken into 8 pieces. • Skin and quarter tomatoes, removing core. • Halve and clean peppers, then wash and dry them before cutting into strips. • Peel onions and garlic and chop finely. • Heat 3 tbsp oil. Brown chicken pieces thoroughly. Add onion and garlic and continue to fry, turning frequently, until soft. • Add tomato, green pepper, stock, 1 tsp salt and pepper, then cover and simmer for 30 minutes. • Wash and drain rice well before frying in remaining oil in a separate pan. Pour in twice as much water as there is rice, add ½ tsp salt, cover and cook over low heat for 20 minutes or until rice is done. Stir in paprika, put into serving dish and arrange chicken and vegetables on top.

Chicken in Peanut Sauce

Economical wholefood recipe

Preparation time: 50 minutes
Cooking time: 50 minutes
Serves 4

1 chicken weighing 1 kg/2¼ lbs
1 tsp sea salt
½ tsp freshly ground black pepper
25 g/1 oz butter
100 g/4 oz carrots
100 g/4 oz/¾ cup shelled peanuts
2 tbsp wholewheat flour
½ tsp ground turmeric
250 ml/8 fl oz/1 cup hot water
2 tbsp chopped parsley

Cut chicken into 4 pieces, wash and dry them before rubbing with salt and pepper. • Melt butter in pan. Brown chicken thoroughly before covering and cooking very gently for 40 minutes, turning once. • Wash and scrape carrots, then chop very finely. • Coarsely grind peanuts and sprinkle with flour over chicken in pan. Turn pieces in this mixture, fry briefly again, then add chopped carrot, turmeric and water. Continue to simmer for about 10 minutes more until sauce thickens. • Taste sauce for seasoning and correct if necessary. Sprinkle with parsley. • Serve with potato croquettes.

Poached Chicken

Requires time for preparation

Preparation time: 30 minutes
Cooking time: 1½ hours
Serves 6

2 chickens weighing 800 g/ 1¾ lbs each
2 tsp salt
1 celery stalk
4 small onions
1 bay leaf
1 clove
4 medium carrots
4 leeks
4 small potatoes
1 sprig each parsley, celery top and thyme

Wash chickens and giblets, then put into large pot with salt. • Wash and chop celery stalk. Peel 1 onion, spike bay leaf on it with clove, then add to pot with celery. Pour on sufficient boiling water to cover chickens. Bring back to the boil, then turn down heat so that liquid barely simmers and continue to cook in this way for 1 hour. • Skim off any scum that forms during first 30 minutes of cooking time. • Peel remaining onions. Scrape and wash carrots, then cut in 4 lengthwise. Halve white part of leeks lengthwise, wash thoroughly and halve again lengthwise. Peel, wash and halve potatoes. • Rinse herbs in warm water, dry and tie into bouquet garni. • After 1 hour add prepared vegetables and herbs to pot, cover and continue to poach for 30 minutes longer. • Remove chickens from stock, cut into serving pieces and arrange on warmed dish with vegetables. • Strain stock and serve as clear soup beforehand.

Bolivian Chicken

An easy-to-prepare speciality

Preparation time: 40 minutes
Cooking time: 1 hour
Serves 4

1 chicken weighing 1.5 kg/ 3½ lbs
2 garlic cloves
3 large onions
4 tbsp olive oil
600 ml/1 pt/2½ cups hot beef stock
1 tsp salt
2 pinches freshly ground black pepper
½ tsp cayenne pepper
400 g/14 oz tomatoes
1 red pepper
½ tsp dried oregano
1 tsp caraway seeds
5 tbsp fresh breadcrumbs
2 hard–boiled eggs
20 pimento filled olives

Wash chicken and giblets, then cut chicken into 8 pieces. Peel and finely chop garlic. • Peel onions and cut in rings, then cook two-thirds of them in oil until transparent. Add chicken pieces and brown thoroughly. • Pour in half the hot stock, stir in salt, pepper and cayenne. Cover and simmer together for 40 minutes. • Peel and chop tomatoes. Halve and clean red pepper, then wash and dry it before chopping. • Combine prepared tomatoes and red pepper with remaining stock, oregano, caraway seeds, remaining onion rings and garlic. Cover and simmer gently for 20 minutes. At the end of this time stir in breadcrumbs. • Serve chicken pieces together with vegetables and sauce, garnished with sliced eggs and olives.

Chicken in Apricot Sauce

A popular dish from Rumania

Preparation time: 40 minutes
Cooking time: 30 minutes
Serves 4

1 oven-ready chicken weighing 1.2 kg/2½ lbs
2 small onions
500 g/18 oz fresh apricots
6 tbsp corn oil
2 tbsp plain flour
350 ml/12 fl oz/1½ cups hot water
2 tsp demerara sugar
1 tsp salt
3 pinches freshly ground black pepper

Peel and finely chop onions. Wash apricots in warm water, dry and halve them, removing stones. • Wash chicken and giblets, pat dry and cut chicken into 8 pieces. • Heat oil in large, heavy-bottomed pan. Brown chicken pieces thoroughly over medium heat, then remove from pan. • Pour off all but 1 tbsp oil. Sprinkle in flour, and add sufficient water, stirring constantly, to make a thick sauce. • Stir in chopped onion and simmer for a few minutes over low heat. Then stir in apricot halves. Add sugar, salt and pepper, then chicken pieces. • Cover pan and continue to simmer over low heat for 30 minutes longer. • Serve with fluffy boiled rice or mashed potatoes and a salad.

Chicken with Aubergines (Eggplants)

A Sicilian speciality

Preparation time: 1 hour
Cooking time: 1 hour
Serves 4

1 roasting chicken weighing 1.2 kg/2½ lbs
3 medium aubergines (eggplants), approx. 600 g/1¼ lb total
1 tsp salt
1 garlic clove
50 g/2 oz streaky bacon
300 g/11 oz ripe tomatoes
6 tbsp olive oil
100 ml/3 fl oz/⅓ cup dry white wine
½ tsp oregano
2 pinches salt
1 pinch freshly ground black pepper
1 bunch parsley

Wash and chop aubergines (eggplants) (unpeeled), sprinkle with salt and put aside to drain for 30 minutes. • Chop garlic and bacon. • Cut a cross in skin of tomatoes, immerse in boiling water, skin and chop. • Cut chicken into 8 pieces. Wash and dry both chicken and giblets. • Heat 3 tbsp oil in large, heavy-bottomed pan with lid. Brown chicken pieces thoroughly with chopped bacon and garlic. • Add wine and allow it to boil away. • Add tomatoes, oregano, salt and pepper, cover and cook on low heat for 25 minutes. • Rinse chopped aubergines (eggplants) and drain well. Fry in remaining oil over high heat for 7 minutes, turning constantly. Add to chicken mixture. • Wash and dry parsley before chopping finely and sprinkling over dish just before serving.

Braised Chicken with Herbs

Economical and easy to prepare

Preparation time: 45 minutes
Cooking time: 30 minutes
Serves 4

1 chicken weighing 1.2 kg/2½ lbs
50 g/2 oz butter
½ tsp salt
2 pinches freshly ground black pepper
Juice of ½ lemon
100 ml/3 fl oz/⅓ cup dry white wine
3 tbsp chicken stock
5 shallots
Bunch parsley
5 sprigs basil
1 lemon

Wash and dry chicken and giblets. Cut chicken into 8 pieces and brown thoroughly in butter over low heat. Season with salt and pepper, sprinkle with lemon juice and add half the wine. • Cover and simmer chicken and giblets for 30 minutes, turning several times and adding stock as necessary. • Peel shallots and chop finely with washed parsley and basil leaves. • Wash lemon in warm water, dry and cut into 8 segments. • Remove chicken from pan and keep warm. • Finely chop liver, rejecting rest of giblets. • Cook shallots in braising juices, without browning. • Add chopped liver and remaining wine, then reduce to a thick sauce. • Reheat chicken in sauce, sprinkle with chopped parsley and serve garnished with lemon segments and basil leaves.

Chicken and Fennel Risotto

Easy to prepare

Preparation time: 30 minutes
Cooking time: 20 minutes
Serves 4

1 kg/2¼ lbs chicken breast fillets
1 tsp salt
Pinch white pepper
½ tsp dried tarragon
750 g/1¾ lbs fennel
2 onions
1 large garlic clove
6 tbsp olive oil
300 g/11 oz/2 cups short-grain rice
600 ml/1 pt/2½ cups chicken stock
250 ml/8 fl oz/1 cup dry white wine
½ tsp salt
50 g/2 oz freshly grated Parmesan cheese

Wash and pat dry chicken fillets, then cut in half and rub well with salt, pepper and tarragon. • Cut off some green tops from fennel, wash and put aside. Trim fennel stalks, quarter heads and wash. • Peel and chop onions and garlic. • Heat oil and brown chicken fillets well on both sides. Add fennel, onions and garlic and fry briefly together. • Wash rice in sieve, drain well and dry. Add to pan with chicken and sauté, stirring constantly, for a few minutes. Pour chicken stock and white wine over mixture, season with salt, cover and cook for 20 minutes. • Chop fennel leaves finely and scatter over risotto with Parmesan cheese.

Tip: The final touch can be given to this risotto with the addition of 50 g/2 oz/¼ cup toasted pine kernels.

Chicken with Olives

Easy to prepare

Preparation time: 25 minutes
Cooking time: 30 minutes
Serves 4

1 chicken weighing 1.2 kg/2½ lbs
1 sprig rosemary
2 garlic cloves
2 ripe tomatoes
16 black or pimento filled olives
4 tbsp olive oil
1 tsp salt
Pinch freshly ground black pepper
3 tbsp chicken stock
2 sprigs basil

Cut the chicken into 8 pieces; rinse thoroughly and pat dry. • Wash and dry rosemary, removing leaves from stalk. Peel garlic and chop finely with rosemary. • Slit round end of tomatoes crosswise, immerse in boiling water, remove skin and core, then cut in pieces. Stone olives. • Heat oil in large, heavy-bottomed pan with lid. Brown chicken pieces thoroughly and evenly over medium heat, sprinkle on garlic and rosemary mixture and continue to fry briefly. • Season with salt and pepper, cover pan and braise gently for 15 minutes on low heat. • Add tomato pieces, olives and stock, simmer for 15 minutes longer, adding more stock if necessary. • Wash and dry basil leaves. Garnish chicken before serving. • Fried polenta or crusty French bread are good with this dish.

Chicken Soufflé

Slightly more difficult

Preparation time: 20 minutes
Cooking time: 1 hour
Serves 4

600 g/1¼ lbs chicken breasts (with bone)
1 small bay leaf
½ tsp white peppercorns
1 tsp salt
2 sprigs parsley
½ tsp tarragon
250 ml/8 fl oz/1 cup water
4 shallots
40 g/1½ oz butter
2 tbsp plain flour
6 tbsp single (light) cream
4 tbsp dry white wine
2 pinches each white pepper and salt
4 eggs
1 tbsp grated Parmesan cheese
Butter for greasing soufflé dish

Wash chicken breasts, put into boiling water together with bay leaf, peppercorns, salt, parsley and tarragon. Cover and simmer gently for 30 minutes. • Take meat off bone and cut into thin slivers. Strain stock. • Peel and chop shallots, then fry until transparent in butter. Sprinkle on flour, continuing to fry until light brown. Add stock gradually, then cream and white wine. Stir well while bringing to the boil. Season to taste with salt and pepper. • Preheat oven to 200°C/400°F/Gas Mark 6. Butter large soufflé dish well. • Separate eggs. Stir egg yolks, cheese and chicken into sauce. • Beat egg whites until very stiff and fold carefully into mixture. Spoon quickly into prepared dish and bake in centre of oven for 30 minutes. Serve immediately.

Drumsticks with Mushrooms

Easy to prepare

Preparation time: 40 minutes
Cooking time: 30 minutes
Serves 4

8 chicken drumsticks
4 tbsp plain flour
2 small onions
1 garlic clove
25 g/1 oz butter
4 tbsp olive oil
1 tbsp tomato purée (paste)
100 ml/3 fl oz/⅓ cup dry red wine
1 tsp salt
2 pinches white pepper
Pinch each marjoram and thyme
Bunch parsley
350 g/12 oz button mushrooms
Juice of ½ lemon
1 tbsp wine vinegar

Wash drumsticks and coat with flour. • Peel and chop onion and garlic. • Heat butter with 1 tbsp oil. Brown drumsticks, adding onion and garlic and frying until soft. • Combine tomato paste with red wine, salt, pepper, marjoram and thyme, add to chicken and cook gently for 30 minutes. • Wash and finely chop parsley. Clean and trim mushrooms, then sprinkle with lemon juice. • Heat remaining oil in separate pan. Fry half of parsley and all mushrooms in it, cooking until all juices have evaporated. • Add mushroom mixture to chicken, sprinkle with vinegar and remaining parsley before serving.

Szechwan Chicken

A speciality from China

Preparation time: 1 hour
Cooking time: 15 minutes
Serves 4

1 chicken weighing 1 kg/2¼ lbs
3 tbsp light soy sauce
2 tsp cornflour
3 carrots
4 spring onions
1 hot red chilli (fresh)
4 tbsp oil

Wash and pat dry chicken, then split in half and bone. • Cut meat into thin 4 cm/1½ in strips. Place strips in bowl and sprinkle with soy sauce and corn-flour. Thoroughly combine, cover bowl and marinate for 30 minutes. • Scrape carrots under running water. Trim, wash and dry spring onions. Shred both finely.

Wash chilli in warm water, dry, remove stalk and seeds before cutting into fine rings. • Heat 2 tbsp oil in wok. Fry chicken strips for 5 minutes, turning continuously, then remove from wok. • Heat remaining oil in wok and fry vegetables for 6 minutes, again stirring constantly. Add meat and stir-fry together for 2 minutes longer. • Serve with fluffy boiled rice and soy sauce.

Chicken Fillets with Cheese Sauce

Quick and easy

Preparation time: 30 minutes
Cooking time: 25 minutes
Serves 4

600 g/1¼ lbs chicken breast fillets
4 pinches each salt and white pepper
1 tbsp plain flour
1 egg
100 g/4 oz/¾ cup blanched almonds, chopped
3 tbsp clarified butter
3 tbsp dry white wine
225 ml/8 fl oz/1 cup single (light) cream
100 g/4 oz Gorgonzola cheese
Pinch freshly grated nutmeg
Pinch sugar

Wash and dry chicken fillets, then rub salt and pepper into both sides. Coat fillets first in flour, then in lightly beaten egg and finally in chopped almonds. Press coating firmly onto chicken. • Heat clarified butter in pan. Fry chicken fillets for about 4 minutes on each side over a medium heat. Remove from pan and keep warm. • Deglaze pan with wine and cream, stirring as sauce comes to the boil. • Cut rind off Gorgonzola, mash cheese with a fork and add it to sauce, stirring as it melts. • Season sauce with nutmeg, sugar and additional salt and white pepper if desired. • Arrange chicken on dish with cheese sauce and serve hot. • Ribbon noodles with buttered broccoli or a green salad go well with this dish.

Champagne Fricassée

A taste of luxury

Preparation time: 35 minutes
Cooking time: 15 minutes
Serves 4

600 g/1¼ lbs chicken breast fillets
Large sprig tarragon
2 pinches white pepper
Juice of ½ lemon
2 shallots
200 g/7 oz large prawns, peeled
50 g/2 oz butter
200 ml/7 fl oz/1 cup single (light) cream
1 egg yolk
100 ml/3 fl oz/⅓ cup champagne
1 tsp salt
Pinch cayenne pepper

Rinse chicken fillets in warm water and pat dry. Rinse and dry tarragon before chopping leaves finely. Rub pepper into chicken fillets, sprinkle with chopped tarragon and lemon juice, cover and marinate for 10 minutes. • Peel and chop shallots. • Rinse and pat dry prawns, removing black vein if necessary. • Take chicken out of marinade and dry thoroughly. Put marinade aside. Cut chicken into strips 1 cm/½ in wide. • Heat butter in large heavy-bottomed pan until foamy, then fry chicken strips for 4 minutes, turning frequently so that they brown evenly. Add shallots and fry for 1 minute more. • Add prawns and continue to fry, turning constantly, for another minute. • Beat cream with egg yolk, stir into fricassée and heat through gently, without allowing mixture to boil. Pour in champagne and reheat, again not allowing fricassee to boil. • Season well with salt, cayenne pepper and marinade. • Serve with green ribbon noodles or potato croquettes and buttered peas.

Braised Partridge with Lentils

An unusual dinner party dish

Soaking time: 30 minutes
Preparation time: 50 minutes
Cooking time: 1½ hours
Serves 4

2 partridges weighing 500 g/18 oz each
250 g/9 oz/1½ cups lentils
1 leek, white part only
150 g/5 oz carrots
150 g/5 oz bacon
2 cloves
1 bay leaf
1 tsp salt
2 pinches white pepper
3 small onions weighing 50 g/ 2 oz each
4 tbsp dry white wine
250 ml/8 fl oz/1 cup chicken stock
125 ml/4 fl oz/½ cup soured cream

Put lentils into large bowl of water and pick over, tipping out floating dirt and rejects. Pour lentils into sieve, rinse well and drain thoroughly. Then put into pot, cover with water and leave to soak for 30 minutes. • Halve leek lengthwise, wash and dry, then cut into julienne strips. Scrape carrots under running water, dry and cut in rings. Cut rind off bacon. • Add prepared leek and carrots together with bacon rind to lentils and water, cover and simmer gently for 1½ hours. Add cloves and bay leaf after first 30 minutes. • Wash partridges inside and out, then dry and rub inside with salt, outside with pepper. Peel onions and cut into eighths. Cut bacon into ½ cm/¼ in pieces. • Fry bacon pieces in large pan until crisp and golden, then remove from pan. • Preheat oven to 200°C/400°F/Gas Mark 6. • Brown partridges all over in bacon fat. Remove from pan and put side by side into casserole, sprinkle with bacon fat and surround with onion pieces. • Roast for 30 minutes in centre of oven. • After 30 minutes, reduce temperature to 175°C/325°F/Gas Mark 3. Pour wine and stock over partridges, cover and continue to cook for 45 minutes more. • Once all cooking liquid has been absorbed by lentils, remove bay leaf, cloves and bacon rind. Season lentils with salt and pepper, then arrange in deep serving dish and keep warm. • Halve partridges and arrange on top of lentils. • Combine cooking juices from game with soured cream in small pan and reduce until smooth and creamy, stirring frequently. Pour sauce over partridges. • Reheat bacon pieces briefly in pan, then scatter over partridges. • Serve with mashed potatoes and onion wedges browned in butter.

Guinea Fowl à la Normande

A speciality from France

Preparation time: 50 minutes
Cooking time: 55 minutes
Serves 4

2 guinea fowl weighing 800 g/1¾ lbs each	
1 tsp salt	
Pinch white pepper	
3 tbsp oil	
50 g/2 oz/½ cup shelled walnuts	
½ tsp thyme	
200 ml/7 fl oz/1 cup cider	
250 ml/8 fl oz/1 cup soured cream	
6 tbsp Calvados	
2 thin rashers streaky bacon	
500 g/18 oz firm, tart apples	
40 g/1½ oz butter	
1 tsp sugar	

Preheat oven to 200°C/400°F/ Gas Mark 6. • Wash and dry guinea fowl, then rub well with salt and pepper. Brown quickly in oil in flameproof casserole, remove from pan and pour off all except 1 tbsp of fat. • Put walnuts and thyme into pan and fry, stirring, for 1 minute before slowly adding cider, soured cream and Calvados. Lay guinea fowl in sauce, covering breasts with 1 bacon rasher each. Cover and cook in oven for 45 minutes. • Peel, core and slice apples. Melt butter, fry apple slices gently for 10 minutes, then sprinkle with sugar. • Brown guinea fowl on wire rack in oven for 10 minutes, and reduce sauce. • Halve guinea fowl and serve with sauce, garnished with apple slices.

Duck Flambé

For special occasions

Total preparation time: 50 minutes
Serves 4

2 boned duck breasts, weighing 300 g/11 oz each	
350 g/12 oz plums	
2 pinches each salt and freshly ground black pepper	
1 tbsp butter	
2 tbsp brandy	
100 ml/3 fl oz/⅓ cup soured cream	
100 ml/3 fl oz/⅓ cup single (light) cream	
Pinch ground cinnamon	
Pinch cayenne pepper	

Wash and pat dry duck breasts. Remove skin but don't discard. • Wash, dry, halve and stone plums. • Put strips of skin into a dry frying pan, cover and fry until crisp and brown. Take out of pan. • Using fat still in pan, fry duck breasts for 3 minutes on each side, then season with salt and pepper and remove from pan. Cover with aluminium foil to keep warm. • Pour away duck fat. Heat butter in pan and fry plums until juicy without losing their shape. • Heat duck and juices gently with plums. • Add brandy and heat, then set alight. After 3 seconds, put lid on pan. • Keep duck and plums warm on serving dish. Combine cooking juices with soured cream, cream, cinnamon and cayenne pepper, seasoning to taste with salt and pepper. • Carve duck breasts in thin diagonal slices, and scatter with crispy skin. Serve sauce separately. • Good accompanied by potato fritters and a green salad.

Duck with Green Olives

A delicious Mediterranean flavour

Preparation time: 45 minutes
Cooking time: 1 hour
Serves 4–6

1 duckling weighing 1.5 kg/3½ lbs
2 small onions
1 garlic clove
1 bunch each parsley and basil
2 tbsp small capers
3 tbsp olive oil
1 tsp salt
2 pinches freshly ground black pepper
100 ml/3 fl oz/⅓ cup dry white wine
125 ml/4 fl oz/½ cup chicken stock
2 duck livers
250 g/9 oz green olives

Wash duck, dry thoroughly and cut into 8 pieces. • Peel onions and garlic. Wash and dry herbs. Finely chop onions, garlic, capers and herbs. • Heat oil in heavy-bottomed pan. Brown duck pieces on all sides, reduce heat and add chopped onions and seasonings. Continue to fry gently for 10 more minutes, then season with salt and pepper. • Pour in wine and allow to evaporate slowly over a low heat, stirring continuously. Then add stock, cover pan and simmer duck gently for about 1 hour. • Wash and dry livers, remove any fat or membrane, then chop finely. Add olives and chopped liver to duck shortly before end of cooking time. Simmer briefly, stirring well. • Serve with white bread and tomato salad.

Duck with Tomato

Unusual sweet and sour dish

Marinating time: 3 hours
Preparation time: 40 minutes
Cooking time: 1 hour
Serves 4–6

1 duckling weighing 1.5 kg/3½ lbs
2 sprigs rosemary
6 black peppercorns
100 ml/3 fl oz/⅓ cup dry white wine
100 ml/3 fl oz/⅓ cup wine vinegar
2 small onions
600 g/1¼ lbs ripe tomatoes
4 tbsp olive oil
Pinch saffron
1 tsp salt
½ tsp black pepper
5 tbsp chicken stock

Cut duck into 8 pieces, wash and dry them, then put in bowl. • Add rosemary sprigs, peppercorns, wine and vinegar. • Marinate duck for 3 hours in mixture, turning occasionally. • Peel onions and slice into thin rings. Cut shallow cross in tomato skins, immerse in boiling water, remove skins and cores before coarsely chopping. • Heat oil in large frying pan and fry onion until golden brown. Add tomatoes and saffron, season with salt and pepper, then cover and simmer for 15 minutes. • Take duck pieces out of marinade and drain before putting into tomato sauce with chicken stock. Cover again and simmer gently over a low heat for 1 hour, adding more stock if necessary. • Adjust seasoning to taste. • Serve with rice and green salad.

Duck in Pineapple Sauce

Easy to prepare

Preparation time: 25 minutes
Cooking time: 1 hour
Serves 4–6

1 duckling weighing 1.5 kg/ 3½ lbs
1 tbsp corn oil
125 ml/4 fl oz/½ cup pineapple juice
250 ml/8 fl oz/1 cup dry red wine
½ tsp salt
2 pinches freshly ground black pepper
Juice of 1 lemon
1 tbsp cornflour
Juice and grated rind of 1 orange
400 g/14 oz fresh pineapple
1 tbsp pineapple or apricot jam

Preheat oven to 200°C/400°F/ Gas Mark 6. • Wash duck and pat dry before cutting into 6 pieces. Brush with oil, lay in casserole and roast in oven for 20 minutes. • Combine pineapple juice with red wine, salt, pepper and lemon juice, pour over duck and baste with mixture repeatedly during remaining 40 minutes cooking time. • Mix cornflour with orange juice. • Quarter and peel pineapple, remove hard core and cut into wedges. • After 1 hour remove duck from oven and place pieces in warm serving dish. Keep warm in switched-off oven. • Skim fat off roasting juices, then strain juices. Combine with cornflour mixture, bring to the boil and stir in grated orange rind with additional water if necessary. Add pineapple pieces and jam to sauce, season well with salt and white pepper, then pour over duck. • Serve with sweet potatoes.

Wild Duck in Beaujolais Sauce

A speciality from France

Preparation time: 1 hour
Cooking time: 1 hour
Serves 8–10

2 young wild ducks, weighing 1.5 kg/3½ lbs each
1 tsp salt
2 pinches black pepper
1 bunch marjoram
800 g/1¾ lbs celeriac
250 g/9 oz potatoes
Pinch white pepper
40 g/1½ oz butter
125 ml/4 fl oz/½ cup single (light) cream
2 tsp lemon juice
2-3 sprigs parsley
2 shallots
250 ml/8 fl oz/1 cup Beaujolais
50 g/2 oz ice cold butter

Preheat oven to 220°C/425°F/ Gas Mark 7. Wash ducks inside and out, pat dry and rub well with ½ teaspoon salt and black pepper. • Wash marjoram and put half in each cavity. Roast ducks in oven for 20 minutes. • While duck cooks, peel, wash and chop celeriac and potatoes. Cover with water and boil for 20 minutes, then purée in food processor together with ½ tsp salt, white pepper, butter and cream. Season with lemon juice, garnish with parsley and keep warm. • Remove breasts from ducks, carve meat in thin slices and keep warm. Pour off cooking juices. • Return remainder of ducks to oven and roast for 40 minutes more at 200°C/400°F/Gas Mark 6. • Finely chop shallots, combine with wine and cooking juices in saucepan and reduce by about one half. • Season sauce with salt and black pepper and stir in butter cut into small pieces. • Pour half the sauce over sliced duck breast. Carve rest of meat and serve all with remaining sauce, accompanied by celeriac purée.

Turkey Goulash

Quick and easy

Total preparation time: 45 minutes
Serves 3–4

600 g/1¼ lb turkey breast	
2 onions	
1 tart apple	
400 g/14 oz celery	
2 tbsp clarified butter	
1 tsp paprika	
1 tsp curry powder	
Pinch ground coriander	
250 ml/8 fl oz/1 cup hot chicken stock	
1 tbsp cornflour	
75 ml/3 fl oz/⅓ cup single (light) cream	
1 satsuma or mandarin orange	
½ tsp salt	
50 g/2 oz/½ cup coarsely chopped walnuts	

Wash and dry turkey breast, then cut in 2 cm/¾ in cubes. • Peel onions and cut into eighths. Wash, dry, peel and quarter apple, removing core and cutting quarters into ½ cm/¼ in slices. Remove tough strings from celery, trim both ends before washing and drying, then slicing thinly. • Heat clarified butter in large, heavy-bottomed pan. Brown cubed turkey, then reduce heat, add onions and fry for 2 minutes longer. Stir in paprika, curry and coriander, then gradually pour on hot stock. Add prepared apple and celery, cover goulash and simmer over a low heat for 15 minutes. • Combine cornflour and cream, stir into sauce and bring to boil again. • Peel orange, remove pips and skin from segments. Stir into goulash, together with salt. Scatter chopped nuts over finished dish.

Duck Goulash

Rather more expensive

Preparation time: 40 minutes
Cooking time: 1 hour
Serves 6

1 duckling weighing 1.75 kg/4 lbs	
1 tsp salt	
½ tsp black pepper	
1 tsp dried marjoram	
6 tbsp olive oil	
2 onions	
2 tbsp tomato purée (paste)	
1 tsp paprika	
½ tsp dried tarragon	
250 ml/8 fl oz/1 cup dry red wine	
125 ml/4 fl oz/½ cup chicken stock	
300 g/11 oz button mushrooms	
16 black olives	
125 ml/4 fl oz/½ cup single (light) cream	

Wash and dry duck, cut into 12 pieces and rub well with salt, pepper and marjoram. • Heat oil in heavy-bottomed pan and brown pieces over a high heat, then remove from pan. • Peel and finely chop onions. Fry briefly with tomato purée in remaining oil. Add paprika, tarragon, red wine and chicken stock; bring mixture to the boil. • Put duck pieces into sauce, cover and braise gently for 1 hour. • Clean mushrooms, cutting bigger ones in half. Add with olives to duck after 30 minutes. • Take duck pieces out of pan. Reduce cooking sauce by about one half, stirring constantly, then mix in cream. Season well. • Reheat duck pieces in sauce, and serve with dumplings or potato croquettes.

Turkey Wings with Peaches

Economical and healthy

Preparation time: 30 minutes
Cooking time: 1 hour
Serves 3–4

800 g/1¾ lbs turkey wings (3)	
1 small bay leaf	
Small quantity soup vegetables	
3 white peppercorns	
4 pinches sea salt	
200 g/7 oz wholemeal tagliatelle	
2 litres/4 pt/8 cups water	
1 tsp salt	
800 g/1¾ lbs ripe peaches	
50 g/2 oz butter	
½ tsp white pepper	
1 tbsp fresh dill	
1 tbsp chopped chives	

Wash and dry turkey wings, put in saucepan with bay leaf, soup vegetables, peppercorns and 2 pinches salt; cover with water before putting lid on pan and simmering gently for 1 hour until tender. • Cook noodles in boiling salted water for about 10 minutes, then tip into colander to drain. • Immerse peaches briefly in boiling water before skinning them, cutting in half and removing stones. Slice neatly. • Heat butter in pan and fry peach slices for 5 minutes, turning frequently. • Remove turkey wings from cooking liquid and cool. Keep stock for soup. • Take meat off bone, cut into pieces before sprinkling with remaining sea salt and pepper. • Combine noodles, peach slices and meat, heat through gently and serve sprinkled with chopped herbs.

Turkey Ragoût

An easy midweek meal

Preparation time: 45 minutes
Cooking time: 15 minutes
Serves 4

800 g/1¾ lbs turkey breast	
1 large onion	
2 garlic cloves	
50 g/2 oz streaky bacon	
1 large carrot	
1 stick celery	
2 tbsp olive oil	
1 rounded tsp flour	
125 ml/4 fl oz/½ cup chicken stock	
250 ml/8 fl oz/1 cup dry red wine	
½ tsp salt	
½ tsp freshly ground black pepper	
Pinch each dried marjoram and thyme	
1 bay leaf	

Peel onion and garlic, chop with bacon. Scrape, wash and chop carrot. Trim, wash and slice celery. Chop all vegetables very finely. • Wash, dry and cube meat. • Heat oil in pan with lid. Fry onion, garlic and bacon until brown and cooked through. Add carrot and celery and continue to fry briefly, stirring well. Next add cubed meat and brown thoroughly. Sprinkle flour over mixture and stir well, then pour in chicken stock gradually and bring to the boil. Add wine and continue to boil, uncovered and stirring frequently, until sauce is reduced by half. • Season ragoût with salt, pepper, thyme, marjoram and bay leaf, then cover again and simmer over a low heat for 15 minutes longer. • Serve accompanied by wholewheat noodles, mashed potatoes or rice.

Turkey Drumsticks with Tomato

Requires time for preparation

Marinating time: 2 hours
Preparation time: 30 minutes
Cooking time: 1¼ hours
Serves 4

2 turkey drumsticks weighing 600 g/1¼ lbs each
2 garlic cloves
Sprig rosemary
1 tsp salt
Pinch white pepper
3 tbsp wine vinegar
5 anchovy fillets
1 small can peeled tomatoes (400 g/14 oz)
3 tbsp olive oil
1 tbsp capers
2 egg yolks
Juice of ½ lemon
25 g/1 oz butter

Wash and dry turkey drumsticks. Peel garlic. Wash, dry and trim rosemary, then finely chop with garlic. • Rub drumsticks with salt, pepper and rosemary and garlic mixture, pour vinegar over them, cover and put aside to marinate for 2 hours. Turn several times while marinating. • Finely chop anchovies. Drain tomatoes; chop roughly. • Heat oil and brown turkey thoroughly on all sides, then add anchovies. Stir in tomatoes and capers and simmer all together for 1¼ hours, adding some tomato juice if necessary. • Take meat off bone, cut into 3 cm/1¼ in pieces and reheat in sauce. • Beat egg yolks with lemon juice and stir into sauce with butter.

Turkey Steaks with Coriander

Easy to prepare and economical

Total preparation time: 40 minutes
Serves 4

4 turkey steaks weighing 150 g/5 oz each
250 g/9 oz shallots
1 garlic clove
4 tbsp oil
½ tbsp crushed coriander
4 pinches salt
4 pinches freshly ground black pepper
1 small can peeled tomatoes (400 g/14 oz)
½ chicken stock cube
½ tsp sugar
2 pinches cayenne pepper
Small bunch parsley

Peel shallots and garlic. Wash and dry steaks. • Heat oil in heavy-bottomed pan and toss coriander in it quickly. Season steaks with salt and pepper, before browning over a high heat for 1 minute on each side. Remove steaks from pan. • Sauté shallots in remaining oil, adding crushed garlic and juice from tomatoes. • Roughly chop tomatoes and put into sauce, then season with crumbled stock cube, sugar and cayenne pepper. Reduce slightly, stirring constantly. • Put steaks into sauce, together with any juice that has collected. Cover pan and warm through over a low heat for 5 minutes. • Wash, dry and chop parsley, then sprinkle over dish. • Serve with noodles.

Baked and Fried Poultry

Viennese Fried Chicken

Well-known and easy favourite

Total preparation time: 45 minutes
Serves 4

2 chickens weighing 700 g/ 1½ lbs each
1 tsp salt
2 eggs
3 tbsp milk
4 tbsp plain flour
125 g/4½ oz/2 cups fresh breadcrumbs
150 g/5 oz lard
Bunch parsley
1 lemon

Cut each chicken into 8 portions, then wash and dry them. Rub well with salt. • Beat eggs with milk in flat dish, putting flour and breadcrumbs in two other dishes. • Dredge chicken pieces first in flour, shaking off any excess. Next dip in egg mixture, and finally coat with breadcrumbs, pressing crumbs on well. • Heat lard and fry coated chicken pieces a few at a time for about 7 minutes, turning to brown evenly. Drain on paper towel and keep warm. • Wash and dry parsley, cut off stems and fry parsley leaves in small bunches until crisp. Reserve remaining lard for roasting. • Wash lemon in hot water, dry and cut in wedges. • Arrange on warm serving dish, garnished with parsley and lemon wedges. • Serve with a green salad and potato salad.

Stuffed Chicken Legs

A bit tricky, but delicious

Preparation time: 20 minutes
Cooking time: 45 minutes
Serves 4

8 chicken legs weighing 175 g/6 oz each
150 g/5 oz button mushrooms
Bunch parsley
2 garlic cloves
50 g/2 oz butter
½ tsp lemon juice
½ tsp salt
Pinch freshly ground black pepper
2 tbsp oil

Clean and wipe mushrooms. Wash and dry parsley, then remove stalks. Peel garlic. • Put mushrooms, parsley, garlic, butter and lemon juice in liquidiser and blend to a smooth paste. • Preheat oven to 250°C/475°F/Gas Mark 9. • Wash and dry chicken legs. Loosen skin from meat, working from thick end and pushing skin up towards bone. Spread filling over meat and pull skin down over it again. Rub pieces well with salt and pepper, brush with oil and lay on rack over roasting pan. Roast for 35 minutes in centre of oven. • Serve with roast potatoes prepared in the following way: peel and halve potatoes, put in roasting pan and scatter mixture of chopped fresh thyme, salt and oil over. Place rack with chicken legs above potatoes so that fat and juices drip down and flavour them.

Chicken Strudel

An Austrian speciality

Preparation time: 1½ hours
Baking time: 30 minutes
Serves 6–8

2 chickens weighing 1 kg/2¼ lbs
100 g/4 oz smoked bacon
2 tsp salt
2 pinches freshly ground black pepper
1 tsp dried thyme
1 tsp dried sage
100 g/4 oz button mushrooms
10 large leaves Savoy cabbage
2 eggs
2 tbsp freshly chopped parsley
125 ml/4 fl oz/½ cup single (light) cream
1 tbsp clarified butter
For the pastry:
300 g/11 oz/2¾ cups plain flour
1 egg
2 pinches salt
125 ml/4 fl oz/½ cup lukewarm water
1 tbsp oil
Flour for rolling out
6 tbsp clarified butter for glaze

S kin chickens, remove breast portions and put to one side. Bone what is left and cut meat into small pieces. • Cut any remaining fat and skin from 2 livers, then wash, dry and chop. • Cut bacon into 1 cm/⅓ in rashers. Put prepared chicken and bacon on a plate, sprinkle with salt, pepper, thyme and sage, then place in refrigerator for 30 minutes. • Clean, wipe and slice mushrooms thinly. Wash cabbage leaves, cutting away thick stems. • Sift flour onto pastry board, add 1 egg, salt, and half the water and knead to smooth dough, adding more water if necessary. When kneaded sufficiently, the pastry should have a dull sheen. Shape into a ball, brush with oil, invert a bowl over pastry and let sit for 30 minutes. • Mince chilled chicken and bacon (still keeping breasts apart) very finely. • Put minced meat into bowl set in another bowl containing ice cubes. Combine thoroughly with 2 eggs, parsley and cream, season well with salt and pepper, cover and put in refrigerator for 30 minutes. • Melt 1 tbsp clarified butter. Cut chicken breasts into 2 cm/¾ in wide strips before frying together with chopped liver over high heat for 2 minutes, turning constantly. Put to one side. • Roll out dough on floured surface into large, paper-thin rectangle. Cut off any thick edges and brush with melted clarified butter all over. • Preheat oven to 200°C/400°F/Gas Mark 6. • Spread cabbage leaves with one half of chicken mincemeat; arrange chicken strips and liver along middle. Cover with remaining mincemeat, then arrange on pastry and roll it up. • Lift pastry roll onto baking sheet in the form of a horseshoe, then brush with melted butter. • Bake for 30 minutes in centre of oven, brushing several times during baking with remaining melted butter. • Cut chicken strudel into 16 equal pieces and serve while still hot. • A fresh mixed salad complements this dish very well.

Confit de Canard

A speciality from France

Preparation time: 40 minutes
Cooling time: 48 hours
Cooking time: 1–2 hours
Serves 10–12

2 plump ducks weighing 2 kg/4½ lbs each	
100 g/4 oz/½ cup sea salt	
1 tsp freshly ground white pepper	
1 tsp dried thyme	
100 g/4 oz lard	

Draw ducks, if applicable, then cut into 8 pieces each. Wash and dry them, removing and setting aside any fat. • Mix salt with pepper and thyme and rub well into duck portions. Put into large earthenware jar, sprinkle with remaining seasoning mix, cover and leave in a cool place for 24 hours. • Render duck fat down in large, heavy-bottomed pan together with melted lard. Lay duck portions carefully into hot fat before covering and simmering gently (rather than frying) for 1–2 hours. After 1 hour, test meat by inserting a skewer into thickest part of thigh. If juices run out clear, the duck is cooked. • Take cooked meat off bone, put in layers into the well-washed earthenware jar and pour cooled fat over it. The fat should cover the duck by a good 2 cm/¾ in. After another 24 hours, cover earthenware jar with foil and a lid, or a plate with a stone as weight; place in cool basement or refrigerator. • If only part of the duck is used at one time, the fat must be melted down again and poured over the remaining confit. It will keep in this way for about 10 weeks. • Prepare the duck portions for a meal by roasting in the oven at 200°C/400°F/Gas Mark 6 until crisp and brown. • Serve accompanied by red cabbage with chestnuts and potato croquettes.

Stuffed Chicken with Brussels Sprouts

A dinner party dish

Preparation time: 30 minutes
Cooking time: 1¼ hour
Serves 4

1 roasting chicken weighing 1.5 kg/3½ lbs
2 small onions
50 g/2 oz streaky bacon
200 g/7 oz chicken livers
40 g/1½ oz butter
1 tart apple
1 tsp chopped mint
2 tbsp fresh breadcrumbs
1 tsp salt
½ tsp white pepper
1 kg/2¼ lbs Brussels sprouts
125 ml/4 fl oz/½ cup dry white wine
250 ml/8 fl oz/1 cup single (light) cream
Pinch grated nutmeg

Wash and dry chicken. Peel onion, and finely chop. Chop bacon and washed livers. Heat half the butter, fry chopped bacon and onion until browned, add liver and fry for 1 minute longer, then cool slightly. • Peel, core and grate apple. Combine with mint, breadcrumbs and liver mixture, season with salt and pepper. • Preheat oven to 200°C/400°F/Gas Mark 6. • Season chicken with salt and pepper both inside and out before filling with stuffing and sewing up openings. • Sprinkle remaining melted butter over chicken, place in roasting pan or heavy casserole with lid and cook in bottom of oven for 20 minutes. • Clean and wash Brussels sprouts. • Pour wine and cream over chicken, add sprouts, season with salt and nutmeg. Cook for 30 minutes longer before removing lid and allowing chicken to brown during final 25 minutes or so of cooking time.

Grilled Chicken with Mango Butter

Nice and easy

Preparation time: 30 minutes
Chilling time: 2 hours
Cooking time: 30 minutes
Serves 4

1 chicken weighing 1.5 kg/3½ lbs
100 g/4 oz softened butter
3 tsp mango chutney
Juice of ½ lime
Pinch cayenne pepper
2 tbsp oil
½ tsp salt
2 pinches freshly ground black pepper

Combine butter with mango chutney, lime juice and cayenne pepper, blending well. Shape into a roll, wrap in foil or waxed paper and chill for about 2 hours in freezer or freezing compartment of refrigerator. • Preheat electric grill. • Cut chicken into 8 pieces, wash and dry them, then brush lightly with oil and season with salt and pepper. • Grill chicken for 30 minutes, turning at least twice and brushing again with oil. • Divide chilled mango butter into 8 equal rounds and lay one on each portion of hot grilled chicken. • Serve with curried rice salad, fresh pitta bread and a salad of avocado and tomato, or sliced fresh mango.

Tip: If you have no separate electric grill, the chicken can be cooked under the grill in the oven.

Sesame Chicken

Healthy and delicious

Preparation time: 30 minutes
Cooking time: approx. 1 hour
Serves 4

50 ml/2 fl oz/¼ cup boiling milk
1 rounded tbsp cracked wheat
2 small onions
50 g/2 oz/¼ cup sesame seeds
2 tbsp oil
40 g/1½ oz butter
3 pinches each salt and freshly ground black pepper
1 egg
1 tbsp chopped parsley
1 chicken weighing 1 kg/2¼ lbs

Pour hot milk over cracked wheat, cover and leave to swell. • Peel and finely chop onions. • Brown half the sesame seeds in pan without any fat, then add 1 tbsp each oil and butter.

Fry chopped onion and soaked cracked wheat briefly, turning frequently. Remove pan from heat and stir in pinch of salt and pepper, cool slightly before mixing in egg and parsley. • Preheat oven to 220°C/425°F/Gas Mark 7. • Wash and dry chicken, put stuffing into cavity and sew up openings. • Combine remaining salt and pepper with other half of sesame seeds and coat chicken with mixture, rubbing in well. • Heat remaining oil with butter, brush chicken with half of it and lay, breast downwards, in roasting pan. Roast for 25 minutes in oven, then turn breast upwards and continue to roast for 25 minutes longer. • Brush with rest of fat before roasting for final 10 or 15 minutes, basting several times with cooking juices. • Leave chicken to rest for 10 minutes in oven after it has been turned off.

Chicken with Thyme

Easy and healthy

Preparation time: 30 minutes
Cooking time: 1 hour
Serves 4

1 chicken weighing 1 kg/2¼ lbs
50 ml/2 fl oz/¼ cup boiling milk
1 rounded tbsp cracked wheat
1 leek, white part only (50 g/ 2 oz)
40 g/1½ oz butter
1 tbsp freshly chopped parsley
2 tbsp dried thyme
1½ tsp sea salt
½ tsp black pepper
1 egg, beaten

Pour hot milk over cracked wheat, cover and leave to swell. • Wash leek and finely chop before browning gently in half the butter. Add parsley and sauté briefly. Stir in soaked wheat and

milk; bring to the boil. Cool stuffing slightly before mixing in 1 tsp rubbed thyme, ½ tsp salt, 1 pinch pepper and egg. • Preheat oven to 220°/425°F/Gas Mark 7. • Wash and dry chicken inside and out, put stuffing into cavity and sew up openings. • Combine remaining thyme with remaining butter, salt and pepper, rub well into chicken skin. • Invert chicken and roast for 25 minutes. Turn chicken breast upwards and continue to roast for 25 minutes longer. • Roast for final 10 minutes, basting frequently with cooking juices. • Leave for 10 minutes in oven after it has been switched off.

Masala Chicken

A speciality from India

Preparation time: 20 minutes
Marinating time: 2 hours
Cooking time: 50 minutes
Serves 4

2 chickens, each weighing 1 kg/2¼ lbs
2 walnut-sized pieces fresh root (green) ginger
2 garlic cloves
1 tsp salt
½ tsp ground cardamon
½ tsp ground cinnamon
½ tsp cayenne pepper
2 tbsp lemon juice
150 g/5 oz/⅔ cup set yogurt
100 g/4 oz/¾ cup blanched almonds
80 g/3 oz/½ cup seedless sultanas
25 g/1 oz butter
250 ml/8 fl oz/1 cup water

Peel ginger and garlic, place in liquidiser with salt, cardamon, cinnamon, cayenne pepper and lemon juice; blend to a smooth masala paste. • Wash and dry chickens, cut in half and lay, cut side down, in heavy metal pan. Spread masala paste over them. • Liquidise yogurt with almonds and washed sultanas, then pour this mixture over chickens. • Melt butter and sprinkle over chickens. Cover with aluminium foil and leave to marinate for 2 hours at room temperature. • Preheat oven to 200°C/400°F/Gas Mark 6. • Pour 125 ml/4 fl oz/½ cup water around chickens, cover and cook for 20 minutes in oven. Reduce temperature to 175°/325°F/Gas Mark 3, remove foil and roast chickens for 30 minutes longer, adding more water if required. • Serve chickens in the sauce, accompanied by rice prepared with saffron and paprika.

Honey-Glazed Chicken

Easy to prepare and economical

Preparation time: 10 minutes
Cooking time: 50 minutes
Serves 4

2 frying chickens each weighing 1 kg/2¼ lbs
2 tsp oil
2 tbsp clear honey
1 tbsp medium hot mustard
2 tsp curry powder
½ tsp salt

Preheat oven to 225°C/425°F/Gas Mark 7. • Wash, dry and halve chickens. Cut 4 pieces of aluminium foil large enough to wrap half of each chicken. Brush with oil and lay chicken halves cut side down on foil. • Combine honey with mustard, curry powder and salt; brush chicken with this mixture. Wrap foil loosely around chicken, sealing edges well. • Put foil parcels on roasting rack and cook in centre of oven for 30 minutes. At end of this time, open foil up and continue to cook for 20 minutes longer until skin is crisp and brown. • Serve chicken with peanut rice or chips and a fresh mixed salad.

Chicken Wings in Batter

Economical

Standing time for batter: 30 minutes
Total preparation time: 1 hour
Serves 4

12 chicken wings	
150 g/5 oz/1¼ cups plain flour	
½ tsp salt	
Pinch cayenne pepper	
2 eggs	
125 ml/4 fl oz/½ cup beer	
1 tbsp oil	
For frying:	
1 litre/1¾ pt/4 cups oil or 1 kg/2½ lbs lard	

Combine flour, salt and cayenne pepper. • Separate egg yolks from whites. Beat yolks with ale and oil, then stir into dry ingredients. Set batter aside for 30 minutes. • Heat oil or lard to 180°C/350°F/Gas Mark 4 in deep-fryer or chip-pan with thermometer. Preheat oven to 100°C/200°F/Gas Mark ¼. • Wash and dry chicken wings. • Beat egg whites until stiff and fold into batter. • Dip chicken wings in batter before frying a few at a time in deep fat for about 4 minutes on each side until crisp and golden. • Drain on paper towel, then keep warm on dish in oven until all are done. • Serve garnished with wedges of lemon and fresh parsley, accompanied by potato salad with fresh herbs and radishes.

Deep-Fried Chicken

Speciality from the U.S.A.

Total preparation time: 1½ hours
Serves 6–8

2 chickens, each weighing 800 g/1¾ lbs	
100 g/4 oz/1 cup plain flour	
2 tsp salt	
2 eggs	
5 tbsp water	
½ tsp freshly ground black pepper	
For frying:	
1 litre/1¾ pt/4 cups sunflower oil or 1 kg/2¼ lbs clarified butter (ghee)	

Mix flour and salt with eggs and water, to make batter, then cover and leave to stand for 20 minutes. • Cut chickens into 8 pieces each before washing and drying them. • Heat fat to 180°C/350°F/ Gas Mark 4 in deep-fryer or chip-pan with thermometer. Heat oven to 100°C/200°F/ Gas Mark ¼. • Dip chicken pieces one by one in batter and fry a few at a time in fat until crisp and brown, about 8 minutes on each side. Drain chicken pieces on absorbent paper towel before keeping warm on plate in oven. Season with salt and pepper before serving. • Delicious accompanied by a salad of tiny raw peas and sweetcorn with crusty French bread.

Tip: This recipe can equally well be followed using chicken breasts or drumsticks, which are often sold quite cheaply.

Chicken Stuffed with Sweetbreads

Something a little special

Preparation time: 45 minutes
Cooking time: 1¼ hours
Serves 4

1 chicken weighing 1.5 kg/3½ lbs
1 tsp salt
1 tsp dried tarragon
½ tsp white pepper
300 g/11 oz calves' sweetbreads
200 g/7 oz button mushrooms
2 shallots
1 garlic clove
100 g/4 oz beef marrow
1 tbsp freshly chopped parsley
2 tbsp brandy
2 tbsp fresh breadcrumbs
1 egg
50 g/2 oz butter
125 ml/4 oz/½ cup dry white wine
200 g/7 oz/1 cup soured cream

Wash and dry chicken, then rub well inside with salt and tarragon, outside with pepper. • Wash sweetbreads, cut off any fat or membrane, soak for 10 minutes to remove any remaining blood, then cube. • Clean and wash mushrooms, then thinly slice. Peel and finely chop shallots and garlic. • Combine marrow with sweetbreads, mushrooms, shallots, garlic, parsley, brandy, breadcrumbs and egg, seasoning to taste with salt and pepper. Stuff chicken with mixture and sew up openings. • Preheat oven to 200°C/400°F/Gas Mark 6. • Heat butter in heavy-bottomed pan. Brown chicken thoroughly on all sides over high heat before roasting breast uppermost on lowest shelf of oven for 1¼ hours. • During roasting, baste frequently with wine and cooking juices. • Allow cooked chicken to rest on wire rack in oven. • Strain cooking juices into small pan, mix with soured cream and simmer, stirring, until sauce is reduced by half. Serve with chicken.

Guinea Fowl with Lentil Purée

Rather expensive

Preparation time: 15 minutes
Cooking time: 50 minutes
Serves 6–8

4 guinea fowl, each weighing 800 g/1¾ lbs
2 onions
1 garlic clove
50 g/2 oz bacon
5 tbsp oil
300 g/11 oz/1¾ cups red lentils
250 ml/8 fl oz/1 cup red wine
250 ml/8 fl oz/1 cup water
100 g/4 oz/½ cup soured cream
1 bay leaf
1 tsp salt
1 tsp freshly ground black pepper
3 crushed juniper berries
4 thin rashers streaky bacon
Bunch fresh basil
1 egg

Peel onions and garlic, chop finely with 50 g/2 oz of bacon and sauté in 2 tbsp oil. Add lentils, 125 ml/4 fl oz/½ cup red wine, water, soured cream and bay leaf. Cover and simmer for about 10 minutes until soft. • Wash and dry guinea fowl, season with salt and pepper and rub well with juniper berries. Cover breast of each bird with 1 bacon rasher and truss. • Preheat oven to 220°C/425°F/ Gas Mark 7. • Brown guinea fowl in remaining oil before roasting for 20 minutes in oven. • Pour over remaining red wine and continue cooking guinea fowl for 30 minutes longer. • Remove bacon after 20 minutes of this time. • Meanwhile, discard bay leaf and purée lentils. • Chop basil finely and stir into purée with egg, salt and pepper. • Carve guinea fowl and serve on bed of lentil purée, garnished with basil leaves.

Partridge with Savoy Cabbage

Rather expensive

Preparation time: 1 hour
Cooking time: 30 minutes
Serves 4–6

4 partridges, each weighing approx. 600 g/1¼ lbs
1 tsp salt
1 tsp freshly ground black pepper
4 tbsp clarified butter
1 kg/2¼ lbs Savoy cabbage
1 tsp dried marjoram
1 bay leaf
2 cloves
200 g/7 oz small onions
1 large carrot
100 g/4 oz streaky bacon

Wash and dry partridges, then rub well with salt and pepper • Heat 2 tbsp clarified butter and sear partridges thoroughly. Add 3 tbsp water, cover and cook very gently for 15 minutes. • Quarter cabbage and remove hard core before chopping coarsely. Sauté briefly in 1 tbsp clarified butter, add 3 tbsp water, marjoram, bay leaf and 1 peeled onion with clove-spiked bay leaf; cover and braise for 20 minutes until tender. • Cut partridges in half. • Peel remaining onions, and carrot, chop both with bacon and sauté in remaining clarified butter. • Preheat oven to 200°C/400°F/Gas Mark 6. • Put half cabbage into large ovenproof dish, place halved partridges on top, sprinkle with bacon mixture and finish off with remaining cabbage. Pour cooking juices from game over dish, seal well with aluminium foil and cook in oven for 30 minutes longer.

Stuffed Guinea Fowl

A special occasion recipe

Preparation time: 30 minutes
Cooking time: 50 minutes
Serves 4

2 guinea fowl, each weighing approx. 800 g/1¾ lbs
200 g/7 oz ceps or other fresh mushrooms
50 g/2 oz streaky bacon
1 tsp butter
200 g/7 oz chicken livers
2 onions
4 tbsp brandy
1 tsp each salt, dried tarragon and freshly ground black pepper
2 tbsp breadcrumbs
Small quantity soup vegetables
4 tbsp oil
250 ml/8 fl oz/1 cup dry red wine
1 small bay leaf
125 ml/4 fl oz/½ cup single (light) cream

Trim mushrooms before thinly slicing. • Chop bacon, brown in butter together with mushrooms and cool. • Wash and finely chop livers. Peel and chop onions, then mix with liver, brandy, tarragon, ½ tsp salt, ½ tsp pepper and breadcrumbs. Combine with bacon and mushroom mixture. • Wash and dry guinea fowl, fill cavities with stuffing and sew up. • Preheat oven to 200°C/400°F/ Gas Mark 6. • Rub remaining salt and pepper well into guinea fowl. Clean and finely chop soup vegetables. • Heat oil in large, heavy-bottomed pan and sauté guinea fowl for approx. 10 minutes. Pour off oil. Lay birds in pan breast up, add vegetables and roast in oven for 10 minutes. • Add half the wine and bay leaf. • After 30 minutes more, gradually add remaining red wine, basting birds frequently with cooking juices. • Brown guinea fowl on wire rack in oven for 10 minutes longer. • Strain cooking juices, combine with cream and reduce by half. • Pour sauce into serving dish, cut bird into pieces and place on top.

Stuffed Turkey with Chestnut Sauce

Popular and tasty

Preparation time: 45 minutes
Cooking time: 2½ hours
Serves 6–8

1 turkey weighing 3 kg/6½ lbs
1 tsp salt
1 tsp freshly ground black pepper
1 tsp paprika
2 tart apples
200 g/7 oz/1¾ cups chopped hazelnuts
100 g/4 oz marzipan
2 pinches cinnamon
1 tbsp lemon juice
250 ml/8 fl oz/1 cup hot chicken stock
125 ml/4 fl oz/¼ cup white wine
150 g/5 oz chestnut purée (canned)
200 ml/6 fl oz/¾ cup single (light) cream
2 tbsp brandy
Oil for brushing roasting pan

Preheat oven to 200°C/400°F/ Gas Mark 6. Brush roasting pan with oil. • Wash and dry turkey, rub well inside with salt, pepper and paprika. • Quarter apples, then peel, core and chop them. Combine apple with nuts, finely-chopped marzipan, cinnamon and lemon juice. Stuff turkey with this mixture. Sew up openings and truss turkey. • Roast turkey breast side down in oven for 1 hour, basting occasionally with chicken stock. • Turn turkey over and continue to roast for 1½ hours longer. • Put turkey on meat dish and leave to stand in oven for 15 minutes after it has been switched off. • Strain cooking juices and mix with white wine, chestnut purée and cream, seasoning to taste with brandy, salt, pepper and cinnamon. Pour over turkey. • Serve accompanied by red cabbage, roast potatoes or cooked apples.

Chicken with Dried Fruit

A Middle Eastern speciality

Preparation time: 40 minutes
Cooking time: 1¼ hours
Serves 4

1 chicken weighing approx. 1.4 kg/3 lbs
150 g/5 oz/¾ cup stoned prunes
150 g/5 oz/1¼ cup dried apricots
1 tbsp sultanas
350 ml/12 fl oz/1½ cups water
4 rusks
3 tbsp single (light) cream
1 egg
2 tbsp brandy
1 tart apple
2 tsp paprika
2 pinches each white pepper and salt
3 tbsp clarified butter
Small quantity soup vegetables

Bring dried fruit and water to the boil, then drain, reserving water. • Crumble rusks and mix with cream, egg and brandy. • Peel, core and chop apple, before combining it with dried fruit and rusk mixture. • Preheat oven to 200°C/400°F/Gas Mark 6. • Wash and dry chicken; rub both inside and out with paprika and pepper, salting inside only. • Fill chicken with half the fruit stuffing, sew up, truss, place in roasting pan and pour melted clarified butter over. Roast for 1¼ hours. • Wash and chop soup vegetables, then simmer in reserved cooking water with chopped giblets for 20 minutes. Strain stock; add remaining fruit and simmer for 10 minutes. • Keep chicken warm. • Deglaze roasting pan with stock and fruit mixture, and pour over chicken.

Chicken in Cider

A speciality from Normandy

Preparation time: 30 minutes
Cooking time: 45 minutes
Serves 4

1 chicken weighing approx. 1.5 kg/3½ lbs
1 tsp salt
½ tsp white pepper
100 g/4 oz butter
250 ml/8 fl oz/1 cup dry cider
800 g/1¾ lbs carrots
1 tbsp honey
4 tbsp freshly chopped parsley
125 ml/4 fl oz/½ cup single (light) cream
Bunch fresh tarragon

Cut chicken into 8 pieces, wash and dry, then rub well with salt and pepper. • Heat half the butter in heavy-bottomed pan, sear chicken pieces, add cider and cover before braising for 45 minutes. • Scrape, wash and dry carrots; cut into 5 cm/2 in pieces. Heat remaining butter in deep pan, add carrots with a little salt and 4 tbsp water, cover and steam gently for 20 minutes. Allow any remaining water to evaporate, glaze carrots with honey and sprinkle with 1 tbsp parsley before covering and keeping warm. • Arrange chicken pieces on warm serving dish. Reduce sauce by half over high heat, then stir in cream, remaining parsley and chopped tarragon. Taste and adjust seasoning if necessary. • Serve chicken with sauce and carrots, completing the meal with parsley potatoes.

Pigeons on a Bed of Rice

A really unusual dish

Total preparation time: 1 hour
Serves 4

4 pigeons, each weighing approx. 300 g/11 oz	
200 g/7 oz/1⅓ cups long-grain rice	
2 tsp sea salt	
1 tsp black pepper	
50 g/2 oz softened butter	
150 ml/5 fl oz/⅔ cup single (light) cream	
125 ml/4 fl oz/½ cup dry white wine	
1 large onion (approx. 250 g/9 oz)	
800 g/1¾ lbs cucumber	
2 tbsp butter	
2 pinches seasoning salt	
1 pinch white pepper	
2 tbsp fresh dill	

Bring rice to the boil with 500 ml/16 fl oz/2 cups water and set aside. • Preheat oven to 220°C/ 425°F/Gas Mark 7. • Wash pigeons, rub well inside and out with salt and pepper, then spread with a thick layer of softened butter. • Put into roasting pan breast side down and roast for 20 minutes. • Place pot of rice in bottom of oven. • Turn pigeons over after 20 minutes, pour cream over them and roast for 10 minutes more, basting frequently with cooking juices. • Finally pour in white wine. • Switch off oven and leave pigeons there for 10 minutes. • Meanwhile, peel and finely chop onion. Wash cucumber and cut into julienne strips. Sauté both gently in butter until transparent, adding seasoning salt and pepper to taste. Continue to cook gently for about 15 minutes until cucumber is very tender, then combine with rice, cooking juices and dill and spoon onto serving dish. Arrange pigeons on top.

Chicken with Cold Nut Sauce

Quite delicious

Preparation time: 30 minutes
Cooking time: 1 hour
Serves 4

1 chicken weighing 1.25 g/2½ lbs	
1 tsp curry powder	
1 tsp paprika	
Pinch white pepper	
1 tsp salt	
3 tbsp sunflower oil	
For the nut sauce:	
2 slices wholemeal bread	
100 g/4 oz/1¼ cups shelled walnuts	
1 garlic clove	
3 tbsp walnut oil	
1 tsp red wine vinegar	
¼ tsp honey	
2 pinches salt	

Preheat oven to 200°C/400°F/ Gas Mark 6. • Wash and dry chicken. • Combine all spices with salt and rub inside of chicken with mixture. Truss, brush with sunflower oil, lay breast down in roasting pan and roast for 1 hour in oven. • Turn chicken over after 30 minutes and baste frequently with cooking juices. • Switch off oven and allow chicken to stand for 10 minutes. • Cube bread and soak in 4 tbsp water. Grind walnuts. Squeeze bread dry and crumble, then combine with ground nuts. Peel and finely chop garlic. Stir walnut oil, vinegar, 2 tbsp water and garlic into bread and nut mixture; season with honey and salt. Serve with neatly carved slices of chicken.

Pigeon Pie

A Moroccan variation on an old classic

Standing time: 6 hours
Preparation time: 1½ hours
Cooking time: 1 hour
Serves 6–8

Batter:

500 g/18 oz/4½ cups plain flour
2½ tsp salt
350–425 ml/12–16 fl oz/1½–2 cups water

Filling:

6 pigeons, each weighing approximately 400 g/14 oz
½ tsp white pepper
4 onions
150 g/6 oz butter
2 tbsp freshly chopped parsley
2 tsp grated fresh root (green) ginger
1 tsp grated lemon rind
½ tsp ground caraway seed
1 pinch cayenne pepper
¼ tsp saffron
1 pinch turmeric
125 ml/4 fl oz/½ cup white wine
125 ml/4 fl oz/½ cup water
6 eggs
2 egg yolks

Crust:

150 g/5 oz/1⅓ cups coarsely chopped almonds
½ tsp ground cinnamon
1 tbsp sugar
2 tbsp oil

For dusting over pie:

Icing sugar and cinnamon

To make the batter, sift flour into bowl, add 1 tsp salt and enough water to mix to a smooth, almost runny consistency. Cover and leave for 6 hours. • To make the filling, wash and dry pigeons; season with salt and pepper. Wash, dry and finely chop giblets. Peel and chop onions. • Heat 75 g/3 oz butter in large, heavy-bottomed pan with lid; brown pigeons evenly, then remove from pan. Sauté onions and giblets in remaining butter, add parsley and all spices (except cinnamon). Stir in wine and water and bring to the boil. • Put pigeons carefully into boiling stock, cover and simmer for 1 hour. • Lift out pigeons, cool slightly, take meat off bones and cut into fine strips. • Pour half of stock into another saucepan. Boil remainder rapidly until reduced to 50 ml/2 fl oz/¼ cup, then cool and skim off fat. • Heat other half of stock to just below boiling point. Whisk eggs and egg yolks and pour into hot stock, taking care not to boil. Stir continuously. Stir in reduced stock. • To make the crust, brown almonds carefully in 25 g/1 oz butter, stirring constantly; remove from pan and cool, then mix with sugar and cinnamon. • Heat a non-stick pan, and dry-fry a little batter until golden. Make 18 paper-thin pancakes in this way. • To form pie crust, take a double layer of foil, lay on it 6 pancakes overlapping in a circle the same size as large pan. Cover with second layer of 6 pancakes. Place almond mixture in centre of layer, then combine pigeon with egg sauce and pour over almonds, leaving 7 cm/3 in free around edges. Brush edges lightly with a little melted butter and fold as far as possible over filling. Cover with remaining 6 pancakes. • Heat oil with remaining butter in large pan. Slide pie carefully off foil and into pan; fry gently for 10 minutes until nicely browned. • Turn pie with help of pan lid to brown other side, again for 10 minutes. • Combine icing sugar and cinnamon and sift over pie. • Serve with a colourful mixed salad.

Quail Stuffed with Morels

A classic dish

Preparation time: 45 minutes
Cooking time: 30 minutes
Serves 6

6 quails, each weighing 200 g/ 7 oz
50 g/2 oz dried morels (wild brown mushrooms)
4 tbsp dry sherry
1 slice bread
250 ml/8 fl oz/1 cup single (light) cream
1 shallot
1 bunch chervil
1 tsp salt
½ tsp white pepper
250 g/9 oz sausagemeat
Pinch nutmeg
1 tbsp oil
40 g/1½ oz butter

Soak mushroooms in sherry. • Cut crusts off bread, cube and sprinkle with 2 tbsp cream. • Bone quails, except for wings and legs. • Peel and finely chop shallot. Wash, dry and finely chop chervil. • Rub each quail well with 1 pinch salt and pepper. Combine shallot, sausagemeat, chervil, nutmeg, soft bread, remaining salt and pepper with drained whole morels, reserving the sherry . • Stuff quails with this mixture and truss. • Preheat oven to 200°C/ 425°F/Gas Mark 7. • Heat oil and butter in large pan. Brown quails in this before putting into roasting pan, pouring over remaining fat, sherry and cream and roasting on lowest shelf of oven for 30 minutes. • At end of this time, switch off heat and leave quail in oven for 5 minutes longer. • Serve with sautéed fresh morels.

Chicken with Sweetcorn Stuffing

Economical and easy to prepare

Preparation time: 45 minutes
Cooking time: 1¼ hours
Serves 4

1 chicken weighing 1.5 kg/ 3½ lbs
2 ears sweetcorn
1½ tsp salt
1 green pepper
50 g/2 oz butter
100 g/4 oz sausagemeat
½ tsp white pepper
2 tbsp oil
1 carrot
1 onion
1 garlic clove
5 tbsp white wine
5 tbsp chicken stock
100 g/4 oz/½ cup soured cream

Cover sweetcorn with water, add ½ tsp salt and boil for 45 minutes. Scrape kernels off cob. • Wash and dry chicken; chop heart and liver. • Preheat oven to 200°C/400°F/Gas Mark 6. • Clean and chop green pepper, then sauté in half the butter with giblets. Add sausagemeat and sweetcorn kernels, seasoning well. • Stuff chicken with this mixture, sew up, brush with oil and roast for 1¼ hours on lowest shelf of oven. • Peel and grate carrot. Peel onion and cut into eighths. Peel and chop garlic, sauté in remaining butter with carrot and onion until nicely browned, pour in wine and stock and simmer for 10 minutes. Strain and combine with soured cream and serve with chicken.

Turkey Fillets in Puff Pastry

Well worth the effort

Preparation time: 40 minutes
Cooking time: 30 minutes
Serves 6

6 turkey fillets, each weighing 175 g/6 oz
600 g/1¼ lbs frozen puff pastry
50 g/2 oz butter
100 g/4 oz finely minced beef steak
125 ml/4 fl oz/½ cup single (light) cream
2 eggs
3 tbsp freshly chopped mixed herbs (including chervil, parsley and sage)
½ tsp salt
½ tsp freshly ground black pepper
½ tsp paprika
Pinch nutmeg
150 g/5 oz/1⅓ cups ground hazelnuts
1 egg yolk
2 tbsp milk
Flour for rolling out

Remove pastry from wrappings and thaw. • Wash and dry turkey fillets, brown well in butter, remove from pan and allow to cool. • Combine minced steak with cream, eggs and herbs; season well with salt, pepper, paprika and nutmeg. • Coat fillets with thick layer of this mixture. • Preheat oven to 200°/400°F/Gas Mark 6. • Roll thawed pastry out slightly on floured work surface, sprinkle with hazelnuts then continue to roll out until 1 cm/⅓ in thick. • Cut pastry into squares to fit turkey fillets. Place one fillet on each square, brush edges with water, fold around meat and seal well. • Place pastry parcels on cold baking sheet that has been rinsed in cold water and left wet. • Brush pastry with beaten egg and milk. • Bake on middle shelf of oven for 30 minutes.

American Thanksgiving Turkey

A speciality from America, for special occasions

Preparation time: 1 hour
Cooking time: 3–3½ hours
Serves 8–10

1 young turkey weighing 4 kg/ 9 lbs
2½ tsp salt
1½–2 tsp white pepper
Bunch parsley
1 lemon
2 onions
100 g/4 oz butter
6 slices bread
125 ml/4 fl oz/½ cup milk
2 eggs
2 tsp dried sage
½ chicken stock cube
1 tsp curry powder

750 ml/1¼ pt/3 cups hot chicken stock
850 g/1¾ lbs sweet potatoes, peeled
2-3 tbsp oil
2 rounded tbsp sugar
2 tbsp cornflour

Wash and dry turkey inside and out; wash and dry giblets. Rub inside with 2 tsp salt and ½–1 tsp pepper. • Wash, dry and chop parsley. • Cut lemon in half and rub juice well into outside of turkey. • Peel onions, then chop with liver. • Melt half the butter in pan and sauté onions and liver with parsley. Cube bread and combine with onion and liver mixture, milk, eggs, sage, remaining pepper and salt and stock cube. • Preheat oven to 175°C/325°F/ Gas Mark 3. • Stuff turkey with mixture and sew up openings, then truss. • Put turkey into roast-ing pan. Melt remaining butter, stir in curry powder and brush bird all over with this mixture. Use some to grease piece of alu-minium foil and place over turkey. Put at bottom of oven and roast for 3–3½ hours. • At end of 1½ hours, add gizzard, heart and neck to pan, pour on a little hot stock, just enough to keep moist-ened, and baste turkey frequently with cooking juices. • Test to see if done after 3 hours by piercing thickest part of leg with skewer. The juices will run clear when tur-key is cooked. When done, remove turkey from oven and allow to stand, covered with foil. • Turn oven up to 220°/425°F/Gas Mark 7. • Par-boil sweet potatoes, then put into ovenproof dish, sprinkle with oil and sugar and bake in centre of oven for 20 min-utes until well browned. • Carve turkey and arrange on warm meat dish with sweet potatoes. Keep warm in oven after it has been switched off. • Pour off fat from roasting pan. Discard gizzard, but chop heart and meat from neck finely. • Deglaze roasting pan with remaining stock, pour into small saucepan and bring to boil. Add finely chopped meat. Mix corn-flour to paste with 2 tbsp water and thicken sauce with this. Taste for seasoning and serve with tur-key. • Additional accompaniments are cranberry sauce and buttered green peas.

Stuffed Pheasant

Extremely good

Preparation time: 20 minutes
Cooking time: 40 minutes
Serves 2–4

1 pheasant weighing 1.25 kg/ 2½ lbs
75 g/3 oz back bacon
100 g/4 oz Parma ham
6 leaves fresh sage
1 tsp salt
½ tsp black pepper
½ tsp grated lemon rind
4 tbsp olive oil
4 thin rashers streaky bacon
125 ml/4 fl oz/½ cup dry white wine

Wash and dry pheasant. Chop back bacon and Parma ham finely. Chop sage and combine with a little salt, pepper, lemon rind and the chopped bacon and ham. • Preheat oven to 220°C/425°F/Gas Mark 7. • Rub pheasant inside with salt, then fill with stuffing and sew up. • Heat oil in roasting pan. Brown pheasant well on all sides, lay breast side up in pan and cover breast with streaky bacon rashers. • Roast pheasant on lowest oven shelf for 40 minutes, basting frequently with wine and pan juices. Remove bacon 10 minutes before end of roasting time to allow breast to brown. Serve with baby courgettes.

Pheasant in Bacon Sauce

A dinner party speciality

Preparation time: 40 minutes
Cooking time: 40 minutes
Serves 2

1 pheasant weighing 1.25 kg/2½ lbs
1½ tsp salt
½ tsp black pepper
4 thin rashers fat bacon
50 g/2 oz butter
50 g streaky bacon
1 carrot
150 g/15 oz leeks
Bunch parsley
2 juniper berries
2 tbsp oil
5 peppercorns
500 ml/16 fl oz/2 cups water
125 ml/4 fl oz/½ cup grape juice
3 tbsp dry sherry
100 g/4 oz/½ cup soured cream

Preheat oven to 220°/ 425°F/Gas Mark 7. • Wash and dry pheasant. Cut off wings and rub well inside with pepper and 1 tsp salt. • Cover breast with bacon rashers and tie in place. • Heat butter in roasting pan. Brown pheasant well all over, turn breast down and slide onto bottom oven shelf. Roast for 40 minutes. • Remove bacon 10 minutes before end of roasting time, turn pheasant over on back and brown breast. • To make the sauce, chop both remaining portions of bacon; scrape, wash and chop carrot; clean and split leeks lengthwise, then wash and slice. Chop parsley and crush juniper berries. • Heat oil. Sauté bacon, then pheasant wings and giblets as well. Add prepared vegetables, parsley, juniper berries, ½ tsp salt, peppercorns and water; boil for 20 minutes. • Strain sauce through sieve. • Keep pheasant warm. • Deglaze roasting pan with sauce, pour into saucepan, add sherry and grape juice and reduce to 250 ml/8 fl oz/1 cup. Stir in soured cream.

Breast of Turkey with Yogurt Sauce

A speciality from Bulgaria

Preparation time: 40 minutes
Cooking time: 45 minutes
Serves 4

1 kg/2¼ lbs turkey breast on bone
2 garlic cloves
½ tsp salt
2 pinches freshly ground black pepper
6 tbsp sunflower oil
1 yellow and 1 red pepper
200 g/7 oz leeks
500 g/18 oz cucumber
Bunch chervil
125 ml/4 fl oz/½ cup hot chicken stock
250 g/9 oz/1 cup thick set yogurt

Wash and dry turkey breast. • Peel and chop garlic, mix with salt and pepper, then crush and combine with 1 tbsp oil. Coat meat with this mixture before covering and putting in refrigerator to marinate for 30 minutes. • Preheat oven to 200°C/400°F/Gas Mark 6. • Discard stalk and seeds of peppers, wash and chop. Trim both ends of leeks, wash thoroughly and cut into 1 cm/⅓ in pieces. Peel, core and slice cucumber. Wash, dry and finely chop chervil. • Heat remaining oil. Place turkey breast in roasting pan, pour hot oil over it and roast in centre of oven for 30 minutes. Arrange chopped peppers and leek around meat, pour on hot stock and cook for 10 minutes longer. Finally add cucumber and cook for 5 more minutes. • Remove meat and vegetables from pan, put on warm serving dish and return to oven after it has been switched off to keep warm. • Deglaze roasting pan with yogurt, pour into sauce boat and sprinkle with chervil.

Turkey Steaks with Courgettes (Zucchini)

Easy and healthy

Total preparation time: 40 minutes
Serves 4

4 turkey steaks, each weighing 175 g/6 oz

1 kg/2¼ lbs courgettes (zucchini)

4 shallots

4 tbsp sunflower oil

250 ml/8 fl oz/1 cup chicken stock

1 tsp paprika

3 pinches white pepper

Good pinch seasoning salt

Juice of ½ lemon

2 tbsp freshly chopped parsley

2 tsp soy sauce

Wash and dry courgettes (zucchini) before cutting into thick strips. Peel and halve shallots, then slice crosswise. • Heat 2 tbsp oil in large pan, sauté shallots until transparent, then add courgettes (zucchini), cover and braise gently for 5 minutes over a low heat. Add chicken stock, season with paprika and pinch pepper, cover again almost completely, and continue to simmer for 10 minutes longer. • Finally remove lid altogether and cook until almost all liquid has evaporated. • Flatten steaks slightly and rub well with remaining pepper. • Heat remaining oil in a large pan and fry steaks in batches for 2–3 minutes on each side until well browned. • Season vegetables to taste with seasoning salt and lemon juice, stir in parsley and arrange on serving dish with turkey. Sprinkle soy sauce over steaks and serve with potatoes.

Turkey Steaks with Sage

Unusual and easy

Total preparation time: 35 minutes
Serves 4

8 small boneless turkey steaks, each weighing 80 g/3 oz

1 turkey liver

4 leaves fresh sage

1 large garlic clove

Piece of lemon zest

50 g/2 oz lean ham

3 anchovy fillets

1 tbsp capers

4 tbsp olive oil

1 tsp salt

½ tsp white pepper

Juice of ½ lemon

Wash and dry sage, then cut into fine strips. Peel and crush garlic. Wash turkey liver, remove any fat or membrane, then cube. Chop lemon zest, ham, anchovies and capers finely before combining with cubed liver and garlic. • Wash and dry turkey steaks. • Heat oil in a large pan, add turkey liver mixture and sauté briefly before laying steaks on top. Season steaks with salt, pepper and sage, sprinkle on lemon juice. Cook for 2–3 minutes on each side, then serve on warmed plate with savoury mixture. • Rice and peas make a good accompaniment to this dish.

Duck and Almonds

Deliciously flavoured

Preparation time: 30 minutes
Cooking time: 1½ hours
Serves 6–8

1 duck weighing 1.75 kg/4 lbs
1 garlic clove
500 ml/16 fl oz/2 cups water
½ tsp salt
250 ml/8 fl oz/1 cup dry sherry
1 onion
125 ml/4 fl oz/½ cup oil
150 g/5 oz/1 cup blanched almonds
1 tbsp cornflour
Pinch freshly ground black pepper
Pinch sugar
4 tbsp soy sauce

Wash and dry duck and giblets. Peel and quarter garlic. Cut neck and wings off duck, place them in pan with water, salt, sherry, garlic and giblets and bring to the boil. • Cut duck into quarters, put into boiling stock and simmer gently for 1 hour on a low heat. • Strain stock, skim off fat, then reduce over high heat to 350 ml/12 fl oz/1½ cups. • Peel onion and slice into thin rings. • Heat oil in deep pan. Sauté almonds and onion until evenly brown, then remove from pan. Put pieces of duck into pan, skin side down, sauté until brown, then keep warm on serving dish. • Mix cornflour to paste with cold water. Use this to thicken stock, season to taste with pepper, sugar and soy sauce. Pour over duck, garnish with onion rings and almonds.

Roast Wild Duck

Dinner party favourite

Preparation time: 40 minutes
Cooking time: 1½ hours
Serves 4–6

1 young wild duck weighing 1.5 kg/3½ lbs
200 g/7 oz ceps
100 g/4 oz streaky bacon
1 onion
15 g/½ oz butter
1 tsp dried tarragon
4 tbsp brandy
Salt and white pepper
300 g/11 oz finely minced beef steak
4 tbsp fresh breadcrumbs
4 tbsp oil
2 apples
125 ml/4 fl oz/½ cup hot chicken stock
125 ml/4 fl oz/½ cup dry white wine

Clean, wash and thinly slice ceps. Chop bacon, peel onion and chop finely. • Melt butter. Sauté chopped bacon to remove fat, then onion until transparent, and finally mushrooms. Season with tarragon, brandy, 1 tsp salt and ½ tsp pepper. Combine this mixture with minced beef and breadcrumbs for stuffing. • Preheat oven to 200°C/400°F/Gas Mark 6. • Wash, dry and stuff duck, then sew up and truss. • Heat oil in roasting pan. Sear duck thoroughly, then place on bottom shelf of oven and roast for 1½ hours. • Peel, core and cut apples in eighths, adding them to roasting pan, together with chicken stock, after first 30 minutes. Pour in white wine after 1 hour and baste duck frequently with juices. • Switch off oven and leave duck in it to keep warm. Remove apple slices with slotted spoon and

serve with duck together with strained gravy.

Duck à l'Orange

One of the classic French recipes

Preparation time: 45 minutes
Cooking time: approx. 1¼ hours
Serves 4–6

1 oven-ready duck, weighing 1.5 kg/3½ lbs
1 medium carrot
1 celeriac
1 medium onion
3 oranges
1 lemon
1 tsp salt
2 pinches white pepper
2 tbsp oil
350 ml/12 fl oz/1½ cups hot chicken stock
75 g/3 oz/⅓ cup sugar
4 tbsp white wine vinegar
4 tbsp Cointreau
2 tbsp cornflour
2 tbsp orange marmalade

Wash duck thoroughly, both inside and out under cold running water, then dry well. • Scrape carrot and celeriac under lukewarm water, then dry and cut into small pieces. Peel and chop onion. • Peel 1 orange, removing all white pith; using a sharp knife, cut down between segment skins and separate pieces carefully. Peel a second orange and the lemon as thinly as possible and cut zest into julienne strips. • Preheat oven to 200°/400°F/Gas Mark 6. • Squeeze juice of lemon and 2 oranges and put to one side. • Rub duck well inside with salt and pepper and truss. • Heat oil in roasting pan in oven. When hot, lay duck breast down in pan and roast for 15 minutes. • Then put chopped carrot, onion and celeriac into roasting pan around the duck. Roast duck for 15 minutes on each side. Finally turn duck over breast side up, pour over hot stock and bake for 25 minutes longer on bottom shelf until done. • Meanwhile, melt sugar to a light brown in heavy-bottomed pan over a gentle heat. Add rind and juice of citrus fruit; simmer gently for 30 minutes. • When duck is done, cut into even-sized pieces and place in shallow ovenproof dish. Switch off oven and put duck back in for 10 minutes. • Pour all fat out of roasting pan, deglaze pan with vinegar, then combine with citrus syrup and simmer verý gently for 1 minute. Take saucepan off heat and stir in liqueur. • Mix cornflour to thin paste with 2 tbsp cold water, stir into sauce and bring to the boil again, then stir in marmalade. Season to taste with salt and pepper. • Pour sauce and orange segments over duck and serve immediately. • Almond croquettes and buttered green beans are tasty accompaniments.

Goose with Cranberry Sauce

A special occasion dish

Preparation time: 20 minutes
Cooking time: 2½ hours
Serves: 6

1 young fat goose, weighing approx. 3 kg/6½ lbs
2 tsp salt
1 tsp black pepper
250 ml/8 fl oz/1 cup cranberry sauce with whole berries
125 ml/4 fl oz/½ cup dry red wine
1 tsp sugar
2 pinches each cinnamon and nutmeg

Preheat oven to 180°C/350°F /Gas Mark 4. • Wash and dry goose, then rub well with salt and pepper. • Finely chop giblets. •

Truss goose and lay breast down in roasting pan. Add giblets and 250 ml/8 fl oz/1 cup boiling water, place on bottom shelf of oven and roast for 1 hour. Then turn over and prick legs in several places to allow fat to run out. • Roast goose for 1 hour longer, basting often with pan juices and adding more boiling water if necessary. • Skim fat off juices whenever possible. • After roasting goose for 2 hours, brush several times with cold salted water. • Bake until juices run clear when piercing thickest part of leg with skewer. • When done, switch off oven and leave goose in it for 20 minutes. • Mix cranberry sauce with red wine, sugar and spices. Deglaze roasting pan with boiling water; strain and combine with cranberry sauce. Bring to the boil and season to taste. Serve poured over goose.

Goose Stuffed with Dried Fruit

Unusual and delicious

Preparation time: 40 minutes
Cooking time: 3½ hours
Serves 8

1 goose weighing 4 kg/9 lbs
100 g/4 oz/¾ cup sultanas
200 g/7 oz/1 cup stoned prunes
200 g/7 oz/1 cup dried figs
2 oranges
2 tsp salt
1 tsp black pepper

Preheat oven to 180°C/350°F/ Gas Mark 4. • Soak sultanas and prunes for 15 minutes, then drain. Wash figs in warm water, dry and chop. • Grate zest from 1 orange. Peel other orange; cut zest into thin strips and reserve. • Wash, dry and chop liver and

heart of goose, before combining with dried fruit and orange zest. • Wash and dry goose, rub well inside with salt and pepper, then stuff with fruit mixture and sew up. • Truss goose and lay on wire rack over roasting pan. Pour 250 ml/8 fl oz/1 cup boiling water into pan and slide into bottom of oven. • Roast for 3½ hours, breast side down basting frequently with pan juices. • After first hour, turn goose over and prick legs to allow fat to run out. During next 2½ hours, brush goose frequently with cold salted water. Skim fat off pan juices whenever possible. • When done, switch off oven and leave goose in it for 20 minutes longer. • Remove pith from oranges and divide carefully into skinless segments. Deglaze roasting pan with hot water and strain. Carve goose, garnish with orange segments and reserved orange strips. Serve sauce separately.

Traditional Christmas Goose

Luxury turkey alternative

Preparation time: 1 hour
Cooking time: 4 hours
Serves 8–10

1 goose weighing 5 kg/11 lbs
800 g/1¾ lbs chestnuts
500 ml/16 fl oz/2 cups chicken stock
3 tsp salt
1 tsp white pepper
500 g/18 oz tart apples
100 g/4 oz/¾ cup sultanas
½ tsp dried mixed herbs
250 ml/8 fl oz/1 cup boiling water
1 tbsp plain flour
½ tsp sugar

Preheat oven to 175°C/325°F /Gas Mark 3. • Cut cross through skin of each chestnut and bake in oven until skins split open. Peel chestnuts. Bring stock to the boil, simmer chestnuts in stock for 10 minutes, then drain and cool, reserving stock. • Wash and dry goose, then rub well with salt and pepper. • Peel, quarter, core and slice apples. Wash and dry sultanas before combining with apple slices, dried herbs and chestnuts. Stuff goose with this mixture and sew up. • Truss goose, place breast down in roasting pan, pour boiling water over it and roast in oven for about 4 hours. • After 1 hour, turn goose over and prick legs well. Then continue to roast for another 2½ hours, basting frequently with pan juices. • After 3½ hours, brush goose several times with cold salted water to make skin crisp. • Remove goose from roasting pan and place on meat dish. Switch off oven and put goose back in for 20 minutes. • Skim fat off pan juices, then deglaze pan with boiling water, strain and add sufficient water to make up to 500 ml/ 16 fl oz/2 cups. Thicken with flour mixed to thin paste with cold water. Season with salt, pepper and sugar. Serve with goose.

Cold Poultry

Turkey Pâté with Two Sauces

An excellent and unusual first course

Preparation time: 1½ hours
Chilling time: 25 minutes (plus 24 hours)
Serves 6

For Paté:

400 g/14 oz turkey liver

400 g/14 oz turkey breast

2 shallots

50 g/2 oz butter

1 tsp salt

2 pinches allspice

2 pinches freshly ground black pepper

2 pinches dried marjoram

2 pinches thyme

2 pinches sugar

2 tbsp Armagnac or port

5 egg whites

1 sachet gelatine (3 tsp)

225 ml/8 fl oz/1 cup double cream

125 ml/4 fl oz/½ cup chicken stock

For sauces:

4 tart apples

1 tbsp sugar

Pinch cinnamon

125 ml/4 fl oz/½ cup apple juice

200 g/7 oz elderberry jelly (from wholefood shop)

Juice of 1 lemon

½–1 tsp maple syrup

Pinch salt

Pinch cayenne pepper

For garnish:

Orange segments, marjoram sprigs and whole elderberries

Cut all fat and skin from livers, wash and dry them, then slice. Wash, dry and cube turkey breast. Peel and finely chop shallots. • Melt half of butter before frying sliced liver for about 7 minutes over a low heat. Keep turning liver while frying, then remove from pan. Sauté chopped shallots in butter until transparent, adding remaining butter and cubed turkey and continuing to fry over a medium heat for 10 minutes. • When breast meat is cool, mince as finely as possible, putting through mincer twice. Finely chop liver and combine with minced meat. Season well with salt, allspice, pepper, marjoram, thyme and sugar, then stir in Armagnac or port. Put in refrigerator and allow to chill completely. • Beat egg whites with 1 pinch salt until stiff. Soak gelatine in warm water. Whip cream until stiff. • Heat chicken stock, then add soaked gelatine and stir well until completely dissolved. Stir frequently while cooling and leave until it starts to set. • Take pâté out of refrigerator, fold in egg whites and cream together with setting stock. Turn into serving dish, smooth top, cover with double layer of foil and leave in refrigerator for 24 hours. • To make the sauce, peel, core and chop apples. Combine in saucepan with sugar, cinnamon and apple juice. Cover pan and simmer gently for 10 minutes, then liquidise or rub through fine sieve. Leave to cool. • Combine elderberry jelly with lemon juice, seasoning to taste with maple syrup, salt and cayenne pepper. • Garnish pâté with orange segments, sprig of marjoram and whole elderberries. Serve sauces separately.

Russian Chicken Pie

Filling and economical

Preparation time: 1 hour
Standing time: 2 hours
Baking time: 30 minutes
Serves 6

Pastry:

250 g/9 oz/2¼ cups plain flour

3 tbsp water

½ tsp salt

125 g/4½ oz butter

Filling:

800 g/1¾ lbs cooked chicken

50 g/2 oz butter

200 g/7 oz/1⅓ cups long-grain rice

1 tsp salt

500 g/18 oz mushrooms

Pinch freshly ground black pepper

3 hard-boiled eggs

125 ml/4 fl oz/½ cup single (light) cream

Bunch dill

Bunch parsley

Glaze:

1 egg yolk

1 tbsp single cream

Butter for greasing tin

To make the pastry, sift flour onto work surface. Make a well in centre and put in water and salt, scattering butter in small dabs around edge. Knead all ingredients together as quickly as possible, keeping dough cool. Roll into sausage shape, wrap in waxed paper and put in refrigerator to cool for 2 hours. • To make filling, finely chop cooked chicken. • Melt half of butter in saucepan, sauté rice briefly, stirring well, then add sufficient water to cover rice. Add ½ tsp salt, stir once and leave to cook for 20 minutes over low heat until all water is absorbed. • Trim and wipe mushrooms, then slice thinly. Melt remaining butter in sufficiently large pan to fry mushrooms; cook over a low heat until all juices have evaporated. Season with ½ tsp salt and pepper. • Peel and chop hard-boiled eggs. • Put rice into a bowl together with chicken, mushrooms and eggs, mixing well and adding cream. • Wash and dry dill and parsley. Cut dill into short feathers, finely chop parsley. Add to filling and season again with salt and pepper to taste. • Preheat oven to 220°C/425°F/Gas Mark 7. Grease tin with butter. • Thinly roll out half the pastry on floured work surface into a circle, a little larger than the tin. Roll out the other half to a circle, exactly the size of the tin. Put larger circle into tin, pressing down well onto base and up sides. Prick base with fork. Spread filling on base and smooth top. Lay pastry lid on top and seal edges together. Prick top to allow steam to escape during baking. • To make the glaze, beat egg yolk with remaining cream and brush over pastry. Bake in middle of oven for 30 minutes until nicely browned. • Serve either hot or cold.

Partridge Pie

Delicious hot or cold

Preparation time: 40 minutes
Baking time: 45 minutes
Serves 4

Pastry:

250 g/7 oz/1¾ cups plain flour

250 g/7 oz butter

1 tsp salt

1 egg

Filling:

2 roast partridges, each weighing approx. 600 g/1¼ lbs

2 shallots

100 g/4 oz button mushrooms

Small bunch basil

300 g/11 oz sausagemeat

2 eggs

1 tsp salt

125 ml/4 fl oz/½ cup soured cream

Pinch each paprika and ground ginger

Flour for rolling out

Make short pastry using flour, butter, salt and egg, knead briefly, then put in refrigerator to keep cool until filling is ready. • To make the filling take partridge meat off bones, leaving breasts whole and chopping rest. Peel shallots and cut into eighths. Trim and wipe mushrooms. Wash basil and remove thick stalks before finely chopping with partridge, shallots and mushrooms. Combine this with sausagemeat, 1 egg, salt, soured cream, paprika and ginger; season very well. • Preheat oven to 200°/400°F/Gas Mark 6. • Divide pastry in half and roll both pieces out on floured surface to form 15 cm × 30 cm/6 in x 12 in rectangles. • Spoon half of filling onto one pastry rectangle, lay breast pieces on top, cover with rest of filling and finish with second pastry rectangle. Firmly seal edges with water before brushing with beaten egg and cutting slits in lid. • Bake on bottom shelf of oven for 45 minutes.

Chicken Liver Terrine

Easy to prepare but requires plenty of time

Preparation time: 1 hour
Baking time: 45 minutes
Serves 6

600 g/1¼ lbs chicken livers, as fresh as possible

100 g/4 oz fatty bacon

2 onions

Sprig fresh thyme

Sprig fresh rosemary

Bunch parsley

25 g/1 oz dried ceps or other mushroom

1 tsp salt

½ tsp each dried thyme, rosemary, ground cloves, cinnamon, mace and ginger powder

5 tbsp medium sherry

500 g/18 oz sausagemeat

200 g/7 oz/1 cup soured cream

2 bay leaves

4 thin rashers streaky bacon

Clean chicken livers of any bits of fat or skin, rinse quickly under cold water and pat dry. • Remove fat from bacon and finely chop. Peel and chop onions. Rinse herbs in lukewarm water and dry, putting sprigs of thyme and rosemary to one side. Discard thick stalks of parsley and chop leaves. Cover herbs and put aside. • Sauté chopped bacon in pan, adding onions and frying in bacon fat until transparent. Then add chicken livers and sauté for 3 minutes, turning frequently. Next add dried mushrooms, salt, dried herbs, spices and sherry; continue to sauté for 1 minute longer, then cool. • Preheat oven to 175°C/325°F/Gas Mark 3. Put 2 litres/

4 pt water into a saucepan and bring to the boil. • Coarsely chop liver, then combine with sausagemeat, soured cream and chopped parsley. Adjust seasoning if necessary. • Spoon mixture into ovenproof terrine. Lay sprigs of thyme and rosemary on top with bay leaves, then cover with bacon rashers. • Seal terrine well with double thickness of foil and place in large pan or roasting pan. Put onto bottom shelf of oven and pour enough boiling water into pan to come to within 3 cm/1¼ in of top of terrine. • Cook in oven for 45 minutes, making sure that temperature of water stays below 100°C/200°F. Check frequently with thermometer and adjust oven temperature accordingly. • Allow terrine to cool in dish. To serve, either cut into slices or use a spoon to scoop out portions.

Tip: Pickles, Cumberland sauce and hot French bread should accompany this dish.

Melt-in-the-Mouth Duck Pie

Complicated but delicious

Preparation time: 2½ hours
Baking time: 1 hour
Serves 6–8

Filling:

2.5 litres/5 pts/10 cups water
3 tsp salt
1 duck weighing 2 kg/4½ lbs
Soup vegetables, carrots, leek, celery, etc.
1 onion
1 bay leaf
2 cloves
100 g/4 oz button mushrooms
65 g/2½ oz butter
3 tbsp plain flour
1 egg, separated
2 pinches freshly ground white pepper
½ tsp dried thyme

Pastry:

350 g/12 oz/3 cups plain flour
150 g/5 oz butter
1 egg yolk
½ tsp salt
250–275 ml/8–10 fl oz/1–1¼ cups iced water
Butter to grease tin
Egg yolk for glaze

To make the filling, bring water and 2 tsp salt to the boil. • Wash duck and giblets, then lower duck, heart and gizzard into briskly boiling water. Put liver aside. Simmer duck gently, skimming off scum as it forms during first 30 minutes. • Wash and trim soup vegetables. Peel and halve onion, spiking bay leaf to one half with cloves. After 30 minutes add vegetables to duck and continue to simmer for 1 hour longer. • To make pastry, sift flour onto work surface with a well in centre. Scatter butter in dabs around edge, putting egg yolk, salt and water in well. Work all ingredients lightly together, then roll pastry in foil and leave in refrigerator to chill. • Remove duck from stock, cool slightly, then take meat off bone and chop very finely. • Skim fat off cold stock and measure out 250 ml/8 fl oz/1 cup. • Finely chop liver; wipe and chop mushrooms. Heat butter, sauté liver and mushrooms before sprinkling with flour and continuing to sauté until pale brown. Gradually add stock and simmer for 5 minutes, stirring continuously. Take pan off heat, stir in egg yolk and season to taste with salt, pepper and thyme. Stir in chopped duck. • Beat egg white until stiff and fold into filling. • Preheat oven to 220°/425°F/Gas Mark 7. Grease a 23 cm/9 in tin with butter. • Roll out pastry into 2 circles the same size as the tin, plus a long strip to make the side of the pie. Place one circle in base of tin and the long strip around the edge, sealing well. • Spoon filling into shell, place lid on top and press edges together with a fork. Prick diamond patterns on top with a skewer so that steam can escape. • Brush with beaten egg yolk. • Bake for 1 hour on bottom shelf of oven and allow to cool in the tin before serving.

Goose in Aspic

A pretty party centrepiece

Preparation time: 1 hour
Cooking time: 2 hours
Setting time: 4 hours
Serves 10–12

1 goose weighing 3 kg/6½ lbs
500 g/18 oz veal bones
2 onions
1 tsp salt
1 piece lemon peel
1 bay leaf
4 peppercorns
4 allspice berries
½ tsp dried thyme
Pinch each dried basil and tarragon
1.75 litres/3½ pt/7 cups water
500 ml/16 fl oz/2 cups vinegar
Good quantity soup vegetables
6 sachets gelatine (65 g/2½ oz)
Large bunch parsley (flat-leaved)

Cut complete leg portions off goose and divide carcass into 4 pieces. Wash all pieces, including neck and gizzard, and put in large saucepan. Wash veal bones as well, and add to pan. Peel and roughly chop onions, adding them with salt, lemon peel, bay leaf, peppercorns, allspice berries, thyme, basil and tarragon to goose. • Bring water to the boil. Pour vinegar over goose, then enough boiling water to cover goose completely. Bring to the boil again, removing any scum as it forms. Cover pan and simmer very gently over low heat for 2 hours. • Trim and wash soup vegetables; add to goose at end of 1 hour. • After 2 full hours, remove pieces of goose and soup vegetables from stock and allow to cool. • Strain stock, then allow to cool before skimming off as much fat as possible. • Cube breast, thigh and leg meat. Save remainder for

other use. Cut carrot and celery from soup vegetables into decorative slices using decorative cutters, if available. • Soak 2 sachets gelatine in 1½ tablespoons warm stock. Add an additional 250 ml/8 fl oz/1 cup hot stock to gelatine, stirring well, then season generously. Refrigerate 750 ml/24 fl oz/3 cups stock. • Rinse out 1.25 litre/40 fl oz mould with cold water and pour in bottom layer of aspic. Place in refrigerator to set slightly. • Wash and dry parsley and break leaves off stem. • Arrange layer of vegetables and parsley leaves on slightly jellied aspic. • Remove 1½ tablespoons plus 250 ml/8 fl oz/1 cup stock and heat. • Soak 2 sachets gelatine in 1½ tablespoons warm stock. Add an additional 250 ml/8 fl oz/1 cup hot stock. Pour over vegetable layer and refrigerate again until slightly set. • Heat remaining stock. • Arrange cubed

goose and remaining vegetables on top of slightly jellied aspic. • Soak remaining gelatine sachets in 1½ tablespoons hot stock, then add remaining hot stock. Pour over goose and vegetables. • Put in refrigerator for about 4 hours to set completely. To turn out, loosen aspic around edge of mould with a knife dipped in hot water. Dip mould briefly into hot water and turn out onto a plate. Serve with salad.

Tip: Save the goose fat skimmed off stock for use in preparing cabbage or pulse dishes.

Chicken and Fennel Tarts

Healthy and economical

Total preparation time: 1½ hours
Makes 6 tarts

200 g/7 oz/1¾ cups wholewheat flour

Pinch salt

Pinch each freshly ground fennel seed, aniseed and white pepper

½ tsp baking powder

100 g/4 oz butter

2 small eggs

400 g/14 oz fennel

250 ml/8 fl oz/1 cup chicken stock

400 g/14 oz cooked chicken

1 tbsp each olive oil, lemon juice and mayonnaise

½ tsp each seasoning salt and paprika

Pinch cayenne pepper

1 lemon

Butter to grease 6 tins, 8 cm/3½ in across

Combine flour, salt, fennel seed, aniseed, pepper, baking powder, butter and eggs; knead the short pastry lightly. • Trim stems of fennel, reserving some of the tops. Wash fennel heads, cut into eighths, then cut again into strips ½ cm/¼ in thick. Bring chicken stock to the boil and simmer fennel strips, covered, for 5 minutes. Then leave to drain in sieve. • Preheat oven to 180°C/350°F/Gas Mark 4. Grease tins with butter. • Roll out pastry and line tins. Bake for 15 minutes, then cool on wire rack. • Chop cooked chicken; combine with fennel, oil, lemon juice, mayonnaise and seasonings. • Cut lemon into thin wedges. • Fill pastry shells with chicken mixture and garnish with wedges of lemon and chopped fennel tops.

Chicken and Grape Tarts

A popular party dish

Total preparation time: 1 hour
Makes 6 tarts

200 g/7 oz/1¾ cups wholewheat flour

1 tsp salt

½ tsp baking powder

2 small eggs

100 g/4 oz butter

400 g/14 oz cooked chicken

½ tsp each salt and freshly ground white pepper

500 g/18 oz green grapes

8 gherkins

100 g/4 oz cream cheese

6 tbsp soured cream

2 tbsp tomato purée (paste)

¼ tsp dried basil

18 leaves fresh basil

Butter to grease 6 tins, 8 cm /3½ in across

Combine flour with ½ tsp salt and baking powder, make well in centre. Break eggs into well and put butter in dabs around edge. Knead all ingredients together quickly. • Finely chop chicken and season with ½ tsp salt and pepper. Halve and seed grapes. Finely chop gherkins. • Using a wire whisk, combine cream cheese, soured cream, tomato purée and dried basil. Add chopped gherkins, grapes and chopped chicken. • Preheat oven to 180°C/350°F/Gas Mark 4. Grease tart tins with butter. • Roll out pastry, line tins and bake in centre of oven for 15 minutes. • Leave pastry shells to cool before filling with chicken mixture and garnishing with basil leaves.

Chicken Croissants

A very popular recipe

Preparation time: 1 hour
Baking time: 20 minutes
Makes 10 croissants

300 g/11 oz frozen puff pastry
400 g/14 oz boneless chicken fillets
200 g/7 oz button mushrooms
2 onions
40 g/1½ oz butter
1 tsp salt
¼ tsp freshly ground white pepper
1 tsp dried thyme powder
2 tbsp single (light) cream
1 egg, separated
1 tbsp condensed milk

Remove pastry from wrapping and thaw according to instructions. • Rinse chicken under cold running water, dry well and chop finely. Trim and wipe mushrooms, and finely chop. Peel and chop onions. • Melt butter in large pan and fry onions until transparent. Add mushrooms, salt, pepper and thyme, and continue to cook, stirring continuously, until all liquid has evaporated. • Take off heat. Stir in cream and leave to cool. • When cool, mix in egg white and chopped chicken. • Beat egg yolk and condensed milk together lightly. • Preheat oven to 200°/400°F/Gas Mark 6. Rinse baking sheet with cold water. • Roll pastry out thinly and cut into 5 squares. Halve each square diagonally, then roll out resulting triangles again to make slightly wider. Put ¹⁄₁₀ of filling along longest edge of each triangle, then roll pastry up to form crescent, bending tips around into semi-circles. Brush with egg and milk mixture and put on baking sheet. • Bake for 20 minutes on bottom shelf of oven until evenly browned.

Quail with Truffled Stuffing

A truly exotic dish

Total preparation time: 1¼ hours
Serves 2–4

4 oven-ready quails
1½ tsp salt
½ tsp white pepper
2 sprigs fresh basil
200 g/7 oz goose liver
25 g/1 oz butter
Pinch each salt and freshly ground black pepper
2 tbsp madeira
2 tsp truffles (canned)
2 tbsp fresh breadcrumbs
2 tbsp clarified butter
½ head endive
2 small seedless satsumas or mandarins
2 tbsp orange juice
1 tbsp sunflower oil
Basil sprigs for garnishing

Wash and dry quails, then rub insides with 1 tsp salt and ½ tsp white pepper. • Wash and dry basil, then finely shred. Wash, dry and cube goose liver. • Melt butter, sauté liver, season with pinch each of salt and pepper. Add 1 tbsp madeira and stew uncovered for 5 minutes. Finely chop truffles before combining with shredded basil, breadcrumbs and liver. • Preheat oven to 200°/400°F/Gas Mark 6. • Stuff quails with mixture, sew up openings and truss. • Heat clarified butter in roasting pan, brown quails thoroughly all over, then place in bottom of oven for 20 minutes to roast. • Pick over, wash and shred endive. Peel mandarins and cut into segments. Combine orange juice with ½ tsp salt, remaining madeira and oil. Pour over mandarin segments and endive and toss. Garnish with sprigs of basil. • Remove quail from oven, cool, then remove trussing string and serve quail arranged on endive salad.

Chicken with Broccoli

A well-known favourite

Preparation time: 1 hour
Cooking time: 30 minutes
Serves 4

1 chicken weighing 1.25 kg/2½ lbs
1 large onion
1 carrot
1 stick celery
6 tbsp oil
3 tbsp sherry vinegar
250 ml/8 fl oz/1 cup water
1 sprig thyme
1½ tsp salt
8 small onions
800 g/1¾ lbs broccoli
1 tsp sugar
25 g/1 oz butter
5 tbsp orange juice
½ tsp white pepper

Wash chicken; cut into 8 pieces and dry well. • Peel large onion and cut into eighths. Scrape and wash carrot, clean celery, then chop both. • Brown chicken pieces in 2 tbsp oil, frying vegetables at same time. Add vinegar, water, thyme and 1 tsp salt, then cover and simmer for 30 minutes. • Peel small onions. Clean and wash broccoli before dividing into florets. • Take chicken pieces out of cooking liquid. Strain stock, then boil onions in it for 10 minutes. Remove from stock. • Boil broccoli for 10 minutes in 600 ml/1 pt/2½ cups water, then drain and cool. • Allow sugar to caramelise to a light brown in butter, add onions and glaze. • Toss broccoli in dressing made from orange juice, ½ tsp salt, pepper and remaining oil. Serve chicken arranged on dish with broccoli and glazed onions.

Goose and Brussels Sprouts Vinaigrette

Easy to prepare

Preparation time: 45 minutes
Cooking time: 40 minutes
Serves 4

4 goose legs, each weighing 350 g/12 oz
1 onion
1 carrot
5 tbsp oil
2 tsp salt
750 ml/24 fl oz/3 cups hot chicken stock
6 tbsp white wine vinegar
6 tbsp medium sherry
800 g/1¾ lbs Brussels sprouts
1 large tart apple
2 shallots
2 tsp lemon juice
Good pinch sugar
1 tbsp chopped parsley

Wash goose legs. Peel onion and cut into eighths. Scrape and chop carrot. • Heat 3 tbsp oil in a large pan. Brown legs over high heat, then sprinkle with 1 tsp salt before adding vegetables and continue to fry. Pour in stock, vinegar and sherry, bring to the boil again and simmer goose for 40 minutes. • Remove legs from stock and cool. Strain stock and boil to reduce to 250 ml/8 fl oz/1 cup. • Trim and wash Brussels sprouts, put in saucepan with 1 tsp salt and water to cover. Boil for 20 minutes, then strain. • Peel, core and quarter apple, then thinly slice quarters. Combine lemon juice with remaining oil, sugar, parsley, reduced stock, Brussels sprouts and apple slices, mixing thoroughly. Arrange on serving plates with goose drumsticks.

Breast of Duck with Chicory Salad

An interesting combination

Total preparation time: 20 minutes
Serves 2

2 duck breasts, boned but with skin, each weighing 300 g/11 oz
2 tbsp clarified butter
1 tsp salt
½ tsp freshly ground black pepper
3 heads chicory
2 tomatoes
200 g/7 oz courgettes (zucchini)
1 onion
1 tbsp lemon juice
1 tbsp maple syrup
2 tbsp walnut oil
1 tbsp chopped chives

Wash and dry duck breasts, then sauté for 15 minutes in clarified butter. Sprinkle with pepper and ½ tsp salt and leave to cool. • Trim chicory, wash in lukewarm water, dry and slice into rings. • Cut a shallow cross in skin of tomatoes, plunge into boiling water, skin and finely chop. Peel and chop courgettes (zucchini). Peel onion and finely chop. • Combine all salad ingredients with remaining salt, lemon juice, maple syrup and oil, sprinkling chives on top. • Carve duck into thin slices and arrange with salad on serving platter.

Larded Breast of Turkey

Great for cold buffets

Preparation time: 40 minutes
Cooking time: 40 minutes
Serves 6–8

1 kg/2¼ lbs turkey breast (in one piece)
50 g/2 oz bacon fat
½ tsp salt
½ tsp freshly ground white pepper
2 tsp paprika
60 ml/2 fl oz/¼ cup light white wine
2 small heads radicchio
Pinch each salt and freshly ground white pepper
200 g/7 oz fresh pineapple
2 tsp lemon juice
2½ tbsp white wine
2 tsp honey

Cut bacon into pieces ½ cm/¼ in wide and put in freezing compartment of refrigerator to become firm. • Wash and dry turkey breast. • Remove cold rack from oven. Preheat oven to 200°C/400°F/Gas Mark 6. • Lard turkey breast evenly with bacon, using a larding needle. Rub salt, pepper and paprika into meat and lay on piece of aluminium foil. Sprinkle with ½ tbsp white wine and seal foil well all around, piercing top several times with a needle. Place on cold rack, slide into bottom shelf of oven and bake for 40 minutes. • Rinse radicchio well without splitting up, arrange on serving dish and sprinkle with pinch each salt and pepper. • Peel pineapple and cut into small cubes, removing hard core. Arrange cubes on radicchio and sprinkle with lemon juice. Heat 2 tbsp white wine, dissolve honey in it and sprinkle mixture over radicchio salad. • Allow turkey to cool, then carve into thin slices and arrange on dish with salad. Sprinkle cold cooking juices over turkey slices.

Larded Breast of Pheasant

A great gamey flavour

Total preparation time: 1 hour
Serves 4–6

2 young pheasants, each weighing 1 kg/2¼ lbs
1 tsp salt
2 good pinches white pepper
2 fresh sprigs sage or 1 tsp dried sage
2 tbsp clarified butter
50 g/2 oz streaky bacon cut very thin
250 g/9 oz chestnuts
2 tbsp sugar
25 g/1 oz butter

Wash and dry pheasants, then rub well inside with salt and pepper. Rinse and dry fresh sage, or crush dried variety. Rub half the sage inside pheasants. • Preheat oven to 220°C/425°F/Gas Mark 7. • Heat clarified butter and brown pheasants over high heat for 5 minutes. Place them in roasting pan, sprinkle with remaining fat from pan, then cover breasts with bacon rashers and roast in oven for 30 minutes. • Cut a cross just through skins of chestnuts and cook them in rapidly boiling water for 20 minutes. • Remove pheasants from oven and allow to cool. • Rinse chestnuts under cold water and then peel. • Caramelise sugar in butter until light brown, add chestnuts and glaze, stirring until they are evenly coated with syrup. Put aside to cool. • Cut breast portions from pheasants, putting aside remainder of birds to be used in other dishes. Carve breast meat with bacon layer in slices 1.2 cm/½ in thick, arrange on serving dish with glazed chestnuts and scatter with remaining sage.

Breast of Chicken with Kiwi Fruit

Quick and easy to prepare

Total preparation time: 45 minutes
Serves 4

800 g/1 ¾ lbs chicken breasts, on bone and with skin
1 litre/1¾ pt/4 cups chicken broth
1 stick celery
1 leek
4 kiwi fruits
1 orange
1 lemon
25 g/1 oz butter
1 tbsp sugar
Pinch salt
Pinch cayenne pepper

Wash chicken breasts. Bring chicken stock to the boil. Simmer chicken in stock for 10 minutes, removing any scum that forms. • Trim and wash celery and leek, then chop and add to stock. Poach chicken and vegetables very gently for 10 minutes longer. • Peel kiwi fruit and cut into ½ cm/⅓ in thick slices. Arrange slices in fan-shaped pattern on serving dish. • Wash orange in hot water, then dry and peel one half very thinly. Finely shred this peel and scatter over kiwi fruit. • Squeeze orange and lemon. • Melt butter and caramelise sugar in it, then add citrus juices very gradually, stirring well. Reduce sauce to 2 tbsp and season with salt and cayenne pepper. • Take chicken off bone, removing any skin, and cut into slices. Arrange on serving dish with kiwi fruit and pour sauce over meat.

Chicken in Tarragon Sauce

Easy to make

Preparation time: 20 minutes
Cooking time: 40 minutes
Chilling time: 1 hour
Serves 4

1 roasting chicken weighing 1.2 kg/2½ lbs
2 garlic cloves
4 tbsp olive oil
2 bay leaves
Juice of 1 lemon
250 ml/8 fl oz/1 cup dry white wine
4 tbsp tarragon vinegar
1 tsp salt
Pinch white pepper
1 tbsp freshly chopped tarragon
12 black olives

Peel garlic and chop finely. Wash chicken, cut into 8 pieces and dry. • Heat oil, brown chicken pieces together with garlic and bay leaves, then sprinkle with lemon juice. Add wine, vinegar, salt and pepper to pan, cover and simmer on low heat for 40 minutes, turning chicken pieces several times. • Remove chicken from cooking liquid, turn up heat and reduce liquid rapidly, then cool. • Arrange chicken pieces on serving platter, spoon on the chilled, reduced cooking liquid and sprinkle with chopped tarragon. Garnish with olives.

Chicken with Anchovy Mayonnaise

Tasty buffet food

Preparation time: 30 minutes
Cooking time: 1½ hours
Cooling time: 2 hours

Serves 6

1 roasting chicken weighing 1.2 kg/2½ lbs
1 bunch parsley
3 sprigs fresh basil
Soup vegetables, carrots, leek, celery, etc.
1 onion
1 bay leaf
1 clove
100 g/4 oz tuna (canned)
4 anchovy fillets
1 tbsp capers
1 gherkin
4 tbsp mayonnaise
1 tsp lemon juice
Pinch each salt and freshly ground white pepper
½ lemon

Wash chicken both inside and out, then place in large saucepan. Wash sprigs of basil and parsley stalks and add to chicken, together with prepared soup vegetables. Peel and halve onion, spike bay leaf on one half with clove and add both pieces to chicken. Pour on sufficient boiling water to cover chicken well. • Boil chicken for 30 minutes, removing any scum as it forms, then reduce heat and poach gently for 1 hour longer. • Drain tuna and finely chop with anchovies, capers and gherkin. Stir this mixture into mayonnaise, seasoning to taste with lemon juice, salt and pepper. Finely chop parsley and add to mayonnaise. • Cool chicken in stock before cutting into serving portions and arranging on platter. • Cut lemon into wedges. Garnish chicken with lemon wedges and serve with the anchovy mayonnaise.

Marinated Chicken Legs

Easy to prepare

Preparation time: 15 minutes
Marinating time: 3 hours
Cooking time: 45 minutes
Serves 4

8 chicken legs, each weighing 150 g/5 oz
2 garlic cloves
1 small fresh red chilli
250 ml/8 fl oz/1 cup dry white wine
1 tbsp Dijon mustard
1 tsp mixed herbs
Pinch freshly ground black pepper
1 tsp salt
6 tbsp olive oil

Peel garlic and chop finely. Remove stem and seeds from chilli, wash and dry it, then cut into fine rings. Combine with garlic, wine, mustard, herbs and pepper to make the marinade. • Wash and dry chicken legs, rub well with salt and place in a flat oven proof dish. Pour marinade over chicken, cover dish and put in refrigerator to marinate for 3 hours. Turn legs several times during marinating. • Preheat oven to 200°C/400°F/Gas Mark 6. • Take chicken legs out of dish, pouring marinade into another container. Brush chicken with oil and return to original dish. Place in centre of oven and roast for 45 minutes, basting with marinade several times. • After 35 minutes switch oven to 240°C/475°F/Gas Mark 9, move chicken up to top shelf and cook there for last 10 minutes so that the chicken legs turn a crisp golden brown. • Allow chicken to cool and serve coated with remaining marinade.

Tip: If more chicken legs are required, they can be cooked in a large roasting pan.

Turkey Breast with Spinach Filling

For picnics or buffets

Preparation time: 1 hour
Cooking time: 1½ hours
Standing time: 6 hours
Serves 8–10

1 turkey breast weighing 1.5 kg/ 3¼ lbs, boned and skinned
400 g/14 oz young spinach
2 medium onions
2 garlic cloves
1 bread roll
50 g/2 oz Parmesan cheese
50 g/2 oz full fat soft cheese
2 tbsp olive oil
1 egg
2 tbsp fresh breadcrumbs
2 tbsp slivered almonds
½ tsp salt
½ tsp dried oregano
Pinch freshly ground black pepper
Pinch freshly grated nutmeg
½ tsp dried thyme
4 tbsp peanut oil
125 ml/4 fl oz/½ cup boiling water
200 g/7 oz button mushrooms
2 shallots
1 bunch parsley
25 g/1 oz butter
Pinch each salt and freshly ground white pepper
275 ml/9 fl oz/1 cup single (light) cream
275 ml/9 fl oz/1 cup soured cream

Pick over spinach and wash it, then place, with no extra water, in saucepan and cook carefully until tender. Drain in sieve and chop. • Peel onions and garlic, then chop both finely. • Soak bread roll in cold water. • Grate Parmesan and chop soft cheese. • Heat oil in pan and sauté onion and garlic gently for 5 minutes without browning. Add spinach and continue to cook, stirring well, until all liquid has evaporated. Transfer to a bowl. • Squeeze water out of bread roll and crumble. Combine with cheeses, egg, breadcrumbs, slivered almonds, salt, oregano, pepper and nutmeg, and stir into spinach mixture. Season this filling well. • Preheat oven to 200°C/400°F/Gas Mark 6. • Sew up cuts in turkey breast where bones were removed. Cut a deep slit in breast to form a pocket. Fill with spinach mixture and sew up. • Rub well with salt, pepper and thyme and put in roasting pan. Heat peanut oil until very hot and pour over turkey. Put in bottom of oven and roast for 1½ hours, pouring hot water frequently into pan and basting turkey with cooking juices. • To make the sauce, trim, wipe and slice mushrooms thinly. Peel and chop shallots. Wash, dry and chop parsley. • Heat butter in pan, sauté mushrooms for 3 minutes over high heat, then add shallots and parsley and sauté together. Season with salt and pepper and take off heat. Stir in cream and soured cream, then cover and chill. • When turkey is cool, wrap in aluminium foil and put in refrigerator for 6 hours. • Carve turkey in slices and serve with the cold sauce.

Turkey Liver Pâté on Wholewheat Crackers

Healthy and economical

Preparation time: 45 minutes
Baking time: 10 minutes
Serves 4

200 g/7 oz/1¾ cups wholewheat flour
Pinch each salt, curry powder, white pepper and paprika
½ tsp baking powder
1 egg
100 g/4 oz butter
Sesame seeds
1 onion
1 tbsp butter
200 g/7 oz turkey liver
Pinch black pepper
3 tbsp single (light) cream
½ tsp each freshly chopped thyme and marjoram
2 tsp freshly chopped parsley
Pinch sea salt
Butter for greasing baking sheet

Combine flour with salt, curry powder, pepper, paprika and baking powder, then make a well in centre and break egg into it. Put butter in dabs around edge and gradually knead all ingredients together. Roll dough into a sausage shape 15 cm/½ in long and 5 cm/2 in thick. • Peel and finely chop onion, then sauté in butter until light brown. Remove all fat and membrane from liver, wash and dry and cut in 2 cm/¾ in pieces. Add to onions in pan and continue to fry, covered, for 5 minutes, stirring well. Then cool, season with pepper and liquidise to a purée together with pan juices, cream, thyme and marjoram. Stir in chopped parsley and season to taste with salt. • Preheat oven to 200°C/400°F /Gas Mark 6. Grease a baking sheet with butter. • Cut dough sausage into ½ cm/¼ in thick slices and sprinkle with sesame seeds. Bake for 10 minutes in oven. • Cool crackers on wire stand before spreading each with a thick layer of pâté and garnishing according to taste.

Mango and Turkey Salad

Easy wholefood recipe

Total preparation time: 50 minutes
Serves 4

3 boneless turkey steaks, each weighing 200 g/7 oz
125 g/4½ oz/1 cup brown long-grain rice
1 tsp cardamon seeds
½ tsp each salt and curry powder
350 ml/12 fl oz/1½ cups water
Juice of ½ lemon
Generous pinch freshly ground black pepper
1 ripe mango weighing 300 g/ 11 oz
2 tbsp soured cream
2 tbsp sesame oil
2 tbsp lemon juice
50 ml/2 fl oz/¼ cup chicken stock
2 tbsp dill
4 tbsp sesame seeds

Put rice in saucepan with cardamon, ¼ tsp salt, ¼ tsp curry powder and water, put lid on and cook very gently over low heat for 35 minutes. • Wash and dry turkey steaks, then sprinkle with lemon juice and pepper. Lay steaks on top of rice during last 10 minutes of cooking time, turning over after 5 minutes. • Drain rice in a sieve. Cut steaks into strips. • Wash mango, then cut into slices lengthwise around stone. Peel the pieces, before cutting some into long thin slices and chopping the rest. • Combine rice with turkey strips, chopped mango, soured cream, sesame oil, lemon juice, chicken stock, remaining salt and curry powder and dill. Taste and adjust seasoning. • Toast sesame seeds in pan without fat, stirring well until browned. Sprinkle over rice salad arranged on serving plate and garnished with dill and sliced mango.

Chicken, Rice and Fruit Salad

Quick and easy

Total preparation time: 45 minutes
Serves 2

200 g/7 oz cooked chicken
125 g/4½ oz/1 cup long-grain rice
½ chicken stock cube
2 bananas
1 tsp lemon juice
150 g/5 oz/⅔ cup thick set yogurt
1 tbsp soured cream
1 tbsp sesame oil
2 tbsp white wine vinegar
125 ml/4 fl oz/½ cup chicken stock with all fat removed
1 onion
1 small red chilli
150 g/5 oz fresh pineapple, peeled
1–2 tsp grated fresh root ginger
1 tsp curry powder
1 sprig lemon balm; optional

Cook rice with water and stock cube in covered pan for 35 minutes over low heat until tender. • Cut chicken into thin strips. Peel bananas, slicing one and sprinkling with lemon juice. Mash second banana and combine with yogurt, soured cream, oil, vinegar and chicken stock, stirring well to a smooth sauce. • Peel and finely chop onion. Cut chilli in half, remove seeds and chop finely. Cut pineapple into small cubes. • Mix rice with chicken, pineapple cubes, sliced banana, chopped onion and chilli, fold in yogurt

sauce and season with ginger, curry powder and perhaps a little salt to taste. • Chop half lemon balm and stir into salad, using remaining leaves as garnish.

Quail Salad

An attractive starter

Total preparation time: 1 hour
Serves 4

| 4 quails, each weighing 150 g/ 5 oz |
| 1 tsp salt |
| 4 black peppercorns |
| 1 stick celery |
| 2 shallots |
| 1 small head radicchio |
| ¼ head endive |
| 100 g/4 oz lamb's lettuce |
| 1 small orange |
| 1 tbsp freshly squeezed orange juice |
| 1 tbsp sherry vinegar |

Good pinch each salt and black pepper
2 tbsp olive oil
40 g/1½ oz butter

Wash quail, put in saucepan with salt and peppercorns, cover with boiling water and bring back to the boil. Skim off any scum as it forms. • Trim, wash and finely chop celery. Peel and quarter shallots, add with celery to saucepan and poach for 30 minutes very gently, making sure water just barely moves. • Wash, pick over and drain radicchio, endive and lamb's lettuce. • Tear radicchio into bite-sized pieces, shred endive and mix the three together. • Peel orange and cut into rounds, then arrange over salad. Combine orange juice with vinegar, salt, pepper and oil for dressing. • Remove skin from quails, cut off breast meat in one

piece and set aside. Chop rest of meat. • Melt butter and sauté quail breasts for 1 minute on each side, tossing rest of meat briefly in hot butter. • Pour dressing over salad and arrange warm quail meat on top.

Chicken and Maize Salad

A good snack or starter

Preparation time: 40 minutes
Cooking time: 1 hour
Serves 4

| 400 g/14 oz cooked chicken |
| 100 g/4 oz coarsely ground maize (polenta) |
| 350 ml/12 fl oz/1½ cups water |
| 1 vegetable stock cube |
| 1 green pepper |
| 1 red pepper |
| 2 medium tomatoes |
| 2 tbsp olive oil |

| 1–2 tbsp cider vinegar |
| 1 tsp freshly chopped rosemary |
| 1 tsp freshly chopped thyme |
| ½ tsp mild paprika |
| Pinch freshly ground black pepper |
| 2 tbsp chopped chives |

Bring ground maize to the boil with water and stock cube, cover saucepan tightly, switch off heat and let stand for just under an hour to swell. • Cut peppers into quarters lengthwise, removing stem and seeds, then blanch for 5 minutes in boiling salted water. Drain and cut into thin strips. • Skin and quarter tomatoes. • Shred chicken. • When maize is ready, combine it with oil, vinegar, herbs, paprika, pepper, shredded green and red peppers and chicken. Mix well. Arrange tomatoes on top and garnish with chopped chives.

Chicken and Asparagus Salad

Makes an excellent first course

Preparation time: 40 minutes
Cooking time: 1¾ hours
Serves 6–8

| 1 chicken weighing 1 kg/2¼ lbs |
| 1½ tsp salt |
| ½ onion |
| 1 bay leaf |
| 1 clove |
| 100 g/4 oz leeks |
| 1 medium carrot |
| 1 small piece celeriac |
| 1 kg/2¼ lbs asparagus |
| 2 tbsp cider vinegar |
| Pinch white pepper |
| Pinch sugar |
| 4 tbsp corn oil |
| 2 tbsp chopped chives |

Wash chicken and giblets, sprinkle with 1 tsp salt, cover with water and bring to the boil. Skim off any scum that forms during first 15 minutes. Then turn heat down and poach chicken very gently for 1½ hours. • Peel onion, spike bay leaf onto it with clove and add to chicken. • Trim, wash and slice leeks. Scrape and wash carrot, then cut into sticks. Peel, wash and halve celeriac. • After chicken has cooked for 30 minutes, add prepared vegetables to pan and continue to cook uncovered for remaining time. • Wash asparagus and peel stems where necessary. • At end of cooking time, remove chicken from pan, straining stock and returning it to pan. Bring back to the boil. Tie asparagus firmly into a thick bunch and stand upright on bases in the chicken stock. Invert another saucepan over top and simmer for 10-12 minutes until tender. Remove from pan. • Take chicken meat off bone and cut into even pieces. • Allow chicken and asparagus to cool. • Mix cider vinegar with ½ tsp salt, pepper, sugar and oil, then stir this dressing into chicken and asparagus. Sprinkle with chives before serving.

Duck and Chanterelle Salad

Excellent as a starter

Total preparation time: 45 minutes
Serves 4

| 200 g/7 oz chanterelles (wild mushrooms) |
| 1 boned duck breast, weighing 300 g/11 oz |
| Pinch black pepper |
| ½ tsp dried marjoram |
| 4 tbsp olive oil |
| 30 g/1 oz streaky bacon |
| 1 small head oak leaf lettuce |
| 2 shallots |
| 4 tbsp white wine vinegar |
| ½ tsp salt |

Clean, rinse and drain chanterelles. • Wash and dry duck breast, rub well with pepper and marjoram, sauté in 1 tablespoon oil for 5 minutes on each side then remove from pan. • Finely chop bacon and sauté in same pan until evenly brown. Add chanterelles and sauté for 2 minutes with bacon. • Pick over, wash and drain oak leaf lettuce. Peel shallots, chop finely and combine with vinegar, salt and remaining oil, then toss salad in this dressing. • Carve duck in thin slices and arrange with chanterelles on salad to serve.

Duck Liver and Red Cabbage Salad

Easy to prepare

Total preparation time: 50 minutes
Serves 4

400 g/14 oz duck livers
Pinch each cinnamon, ground cloves, ground coriander and dried thyme powders
500 g/18 oz red cabbage
1½ tsp salt
5 tbsp red wine vinegar
4 tbsp sunflower oil
1 head lettuce
8 rashers thinly cut bacon (50 g/2 oz)
Pinch white pepper
6 tbsp medium sherry
2 tbsp single (light) cream
1 tsp lemon juice
Pinch each salt and pepper
4 pear halves, canned
4 tbsp redcurrant jelly

Remove any fat or membrane from livers, rinse under cold water, pat dry, then cut into 2 cm /¾ in cubes. Combine with cinnamon, ground cloves, coriander and thyme. • Quarter red cabbage and shred as finely as possible, before pounding for 5 minutes with a rolling pin. • Combine 1 tsp salt, vinegar and oil, then toss cabbage in dressing. • Arrange lettuce leaves on serving dish. • Brown rashers of bacon in pan until crisp, then remove from pan. Sauté liver in bacon fat for 5 minutes, season with salt and pepper, add 5 tbsp sherry and keep warm. • Mix cream with lemon juice, ½ tsp salt, pepper and remaining sherry; sprinkle this dressing over lettuce. Arrange red cabbage over lettuce, with liver, bacon and pan juices on top. Crumble bacon over salad. Fill hollows in pear halves with redcurrant jelly and arrange on salad platter.

Turkey and Barley Salad

Serve as a salad

Soaking time: 12 hours
Preparation time: 30 minutes
Cooking time: 50 minutes
Serves 4

150 g/5 oz pot barley
1 litre/1¾ pt/4 cups water
1 turkey drumstick weighing 800 g/1¾ lbs
2 pinches freshly ground black pepper
Soup vegetables, carrots, leek, celery, etc.
100 g/4 oz/⅔ cup stoned prunes
1 leek, white part only (50 g/ 2 oz)
1 vegetable stock cube
2 tbsp sunflower oil
2 tbsp red wine vinegar
2 tbsp soured cream
½ tsp salt

Put barley and water in container, cover and soak for 12 hours. • Transfer barley and water to saucepan large enough to contain turkey drumstick as well. Wash and dry drumstick, rub well with a pinch of pepper and place on barley in pan. Cover pan and simmer gently for 50 minutes until done, turning drumstick over after 30 minutes. • Trim, wash and chop soup vegetables, then add to turkey for final 15 minutes cooking time, with more water if required. • Drain barley in sieve. Take meat off bone and cut into 3 cm/1¼ in pieces, sprinkling with remaining pepper. Chop carrot and celery finely, discard leek. • Rinse prunes in warm water, then dry and quarter them. Wash and dry leek, then cut into very thin rings. • Bring 250 ml/8 fl oz/1 cup water to the boil and dissolve stock cube in it. • Combine barley with prunes, carrot, celery, leek, turkey, stock, oil, vinegar, soured cream and salt, tasting and adding a little more red wine vinegar and salt if desired.

Potato Salad with Turkey Breast

A good starter or salad

Preparation time: 40 minutes
Cooking time: 30 minutes
Serves 4

800 g/1¾ lbs potatoes
Scant 250 ml/8 fl oz/1 cup chicken stock
2 red onions
2 ripe avocados
2 pinches freshly ground black pepper
3–4 tbsp white wine vinegar
2 tbsp sunflower oil
300 g/11 oz smoked turkey breast
½–1 tsp seasoning salt
2 tbsp fresh dill

Scrub potatoes well under running cold water, put in saucepan, cover with water and bring to the boil. Put lid on pan and cook for 20 minutes until done. • Bring chicken stock to the boil. • Peel onions, cut into quarters lengthwise, then into very thin slices across the quarters. • Cut avocados in half lengthwise; remove pith and peel. Then halve again lengthwise and slice the quarters. • Drain cooked potatoes, rinse with cold water, then peel and chop. Add hot stock and pepper to chopped potatoes, then sliced onions and avocados with vinegar and oil. • Chop turkey breast and stir into potato salad; add seasoning salt. • Sprinkle with chopped dill before serving.

Duck Salad

An unusual combination

Total preparation time: 50 minutes
Serves 4

75 g/3 oz/½ cup pot barley
350 ml/12 fl oz/1½ cups chicken stock
400 g/14 oz Savoy cabbage
1 litre/1¾ pt/4 cups water
1 tsp salt
1 red onion
400 g/14 oz cooked duck, off bone
1 tbsp sunflower oil
2 tbsp red wine vinegar
1 tsp Worcestershire sauce
Pinch freshly ground black pepper

Soak barley in water for 12 hours. Then place in chicken stock, bring to the boil, and boil for 5 minutes. Turn heat down as far as possible and leave pan, covered, for 40 minutes to finish cooking. • Wash cabbage, cut away thick stem and any bad bits before finely shredding leaves. Blanch shredded cabbage for 5 minutes in boiling salted water and drain in sieve. • Peel onions, quarter lengthwise and slice thinly across quarters. Cut duck into thin strips. • Drain cooked barley in sieve. • Combine warm barley with cabbage, oil, vinegar, Worcestershire sauce and pepper, adding a little stock from barley if necessary. • Arrange onion and duck on top of salad shortly before serving.

Celery Salad with Turkey

Makes a good hors d'oeuvre

Total preparation time: 30 minutes
Serves 4

300 g/11 oz celery
2 yellow peppers
400 g/14 oz smoked turkey breast
1 small onion
4 tbsp mayonnaise
250 ml/8 fl oz/1 cup low fat yogurt
2 tsp hot mustard
1 tsp maple syrup
½ tsp salt
Pinch white pepper

Separate celery into stalks, cut off green tops, rinse in lukewarm water, dry and put aside. Wash and dry stalks, removing any coarse strings. Slice into 1 cm/⅓ in pieces. • Halve peppers, remove stems and seeds, wash and dry, then cut into strips. Carve turkey into slices 1 cm/⅓ in thick, then cut slices into 1 cm/⅓ strips. • Peel and grate onion before combining with mayonnaise, yogurt, mustard, maple syrup, salt and pepper. • Toss all salad ingredients lightly in dressing, then cover and allow to stand at room temperature for about 10 minutes before serving. • Serve with crackers and garnish with green celery tops.

Chicken and Orange Salad

Quick and easy to prepare

Total preparation time: 30 minutes
Serves 4

1 grilled or roast chicken weighing 1.25 kg/2½ lbs
2 medium oranges
2 slices fresh pineapple
100 g/4 oz/¾ cup cooked long grain rice
2 tbsp pineapple juice
1 tbsp fresh orange juice
½ tsp salt
2 egg yolks
1 tsp mild mustard
1 pinch paprika
4 tbsp oil
5 mint leaves

Remove skin from chicken and take meat off bone, cutting it into even pieces. • Peel oranges carefully, removing all white pith, then separate into segments. Quarter segments and remove any pips. • Cut skin off pineapple and cut into wedges. • Combine chicken pieces with rice and prepared orange and pineapple. • Mix pineapple juice, orange juice and salt. Whisk egg yolks with mustard and paprika, adding oil drop by drop and whisking continuously until a thick mayonnaise forms. Stir fruit juice into this mayonnaise, then fold into salad. • Rinse mint leaves in lukewarm water, pat dry, then shred and sprinkle over salad.

Tip: If you have enough time available, poach a chicken yourself and use instead of the ready-cooked one, serving the stock as a soup course before the salad.

Turkey Cocktail in Yogurt Sauce

A classic starter

Total preparation time: 1½ hours
Serves 4

1 litre/1¾ pt/4 cups water
1 tsp salt
1 turkey drumstick weighing 1 kg/2¼ lbs
2 bananas
2 apples (Cox's)
Juice of ½ lemon
1 small pineapple
200 g/7 oz black grapes
200 ml/7 fl oz/1 cup double cream
450 ml/¾ pt/1¾ cups thick set yogurt
Pinch each salt and white pepper
1 tbsp brandy
6 sprigs mint

Bring water and salt to the boil, put in washed turkey drumstick, cover and simmer for 1 hour. • Peel bananas, halve lengthwise and slice. Quarter, peel, core and chop apples, then mix with sliced banana and sprinkle with lemon juice. • Slice pineapple, halve each slice, cut away skin and hard core, then cut into small cubes. Wash and dry grapes, then halve and remove pips. • When drumstick is cool enough to handle, take meat off bone, chop and cool. • Whip cream until stiff, then combine with yogurt, salt, pepper and brandy. Pour this sauce over fruit and turkey and mix well. • Garnish with mint sprigs.

Chicken and Fruit Salad

Delicious oriental flavour

Total preparation time: 40 minutes
Serves 4

600 g/1¼ lbs breast chicken fillets
2 tbsp butter
1 tsp salt
½ tsp white pepper
500 g/18 oz strawberries
150 g/5 oz bean sprouts
2 tsp chopped preserved ginger
1 tbsp ginger syrup
1 tbsp basil vinegar
1 tbsp soy sauce
Pinch each salt and cayenne pepper
2 tbsp olive oil

Wash chicken thoroughly, then dry and remove skin if necessary. Cut into strips 1 cm/⅓ in thick. • Heat butter and sauté chicken strips for 8 minutes, turning frequently, then season with salt and pepper before removing from pan and draining on paper towel. Allow to cool. • Rinse strawberries several times in warm water, drain well and hull, halving any big berries. Wash and pick over bean sprouts, then combine with strawberries, cooled chicken and chopped ginger in a bowl. • Mix ginger syrup with vinegar, soy sauce, salt and cayenne pepper, adding oil and tossing salad gently in the dressing. • Cover salad and leave for 10 minutes at room temperature for flavour to develop fully.

Index